KITCHEN
TABLE

100 Recipes for Entertaining

KITCHEN TABLE gives you a wealth of recipes from your favourite chefs. Whether you want a quick weekday supper, sumptuous weekend feast or food for friends and family, let the My Kitchen Table experts bring their favourite dishes to your home.

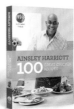

To find out more about our exciting **my** recipe App, get exclusive recipes, read our blog or subscribe to our newsletter, visit our site at www.mykitchentable.co.uk

Throughout this book, when you see **my** visit the website for practical videos, tips and hints from the My Kitchen Table team.

KITCHEN
TABLE

100 Recipes for Entertaining
RAYMOND BLANC

www.mykitchentable.co.uk

Welcome to  KITCHEN TABLE

This book will show you how to create delicious dinner-party recipes – how to turn good-quality ingredients, with a little time and effort, into dishes to impress. I hope many of these recipes will become your favourites.

Raymond Blanc

Contents

Maman Blanc's Vegetable and Chervil Soup

A small tribute to 'Maman Blanc', and I should say to 'Papa Blanc', too, as most of the vegetables would come from his garden. The success of this soup depends upon the freshness and quality of the vegetables used.

Step one On a medium heat, in a large pan, melt the butter and then add the onion, garlic, carrots, celery and leeks. Soften the vegetables for 5 minutes, without letting them colour (this helps to extract maximum flavour). Season with 8 pinches of sea salt and 2 pinches of white pepper.

Step two Add the courgette, tomatoes and boiling water (using boiling water reduces the cooking time and also helps to keep the colours bright). Boil fast for 5–7 minutes, until the vegetables are just tender. Stir in the chopped chervil.

Step three Whisk in the crème fraîche or butter (or both, if you wish!). Taste and adjust the seasoning if necessary, then serve. This soup can be puréed in a blender if you prefer a smooth texture.

Serves 4–6

for the soup

15g (½ oz) unsalted butter

1 onion, cut into 3mm (⅛ in) dice

1 garlic clove, crushed

2 large carrots, cut into slices 3mm (⅛ in) thick

3 celery sticks, cut into slices 5mm (¼ in) thick

2 leeks, 2 outer layers removed, cut into slices 1cm (½ in) thick

1 large courgette, halved lengthways and cut into slices 5mm (¼ in) thick

2 ripe tomatoes, roughly chopped

1 litre (1¾ pints) boiling water

a large handful of fresh chervil, roughly chopped

to finish

1 tbsp crème fraîche or 15g (½ oz) unsalted butter

For a video masterclass on chopping vegetables, go to
www.mykitchentable.co.uk/videos/choppingvegetables

French Onion Soup

The humble onion is very much part of the French culinary anthology. It was probably also responsible for the second invasion of England by the French. I still remember, when I first came to England, seeing Frenchmen riding very drunkenly on bicycles, loaded with magnificent entwined onions. The quality of the onions is crucial in this recipe. We want both high acidity and high sugar levels to create a fully flavoured soup. The best onions are Pink Roscoff; Spanish onions, although lacking in acidity, will also work. If you like a strong onion flavour, caramelise the onions for a further 15 minutes, until very dark brown.

Serves 4

50g (2oz) unsalted butter, diced

4 medium Pink Roscoff or Spanish onions, cut in half and then sliced 3mm (1⅛in) thick

1 heaped tbsp plain flour

200ml (7fl oz) dry white wine, boiled for 30 seconds to remove the alcohol

1.5 litres (2½ pints) boiling water

1 tsp sugar (optional)

to serve

12 x 1cm (½in) thick slices of baguette, for croûtons

150g (5oz) Gruyère, grated

Step one Preheat the oven to 200°C/400°F/gas 6. On a high heat, in a large non-stick pan, melt the butter without letting it brown. Add the onions and soften for 5 minutes, stirring frequently. Season with 10 pinches of sea salt and 2 pinches of black pepper, then continue cooking the onions for 20–30 minutes to achieve an even, rich brown caramel colour. Stir every 2–3 minutes to prevent burning.

Step two Sprinkle the flour onto a baking sheet and bake it for 8–10 minutes, until it is very lightly coloured. Stir the flour into the caramelised onions and mix thoroughly.

Step three Gradually stir in the white wine and one-third of the boiling water. Whisk well and add the remaining water. Bring to the boil, skim off any impurities from the surface and simmer for 15 minutes. Taste and adjust the seasoning, adding the sugar if required.

Step four To make the croûtons, preheat the grill to hot. Arrange the baguette slices on a baking sheet and sprinkle two-thirds of the grated Gruyère over them. Place under the grill for 3–4 minutes to melt and slightly brown the cheese. Serve the soup in bowls, with the croûtons on top. Serve the remaining Gruyère separately.

Butterbean Soup with Smoked Streaky Bacon

In my native Franche-Comté, the pig is as celebrated as a demi-god. This soup is a simple and delicious way to enjoy it. Butterbeans are quite large and well textured. I like them very much in this soup but you could mix in other varieties such as broad, cannelloni, borlotti, haricot or flageolet. The soup needs an hour to cook, so the heat must be gentle. If it is too strong, the beans will break up and release too much starch and the bacon will shrivel and harden.

Step one In a large, heavy-based pan, gently melt the butter – it must not brown – and sweat the onion and garlic over a medium heat for about 5 minutes, stirring occasionally, until soft.

Step two Add all the remaining ingredients, 4 large pinches of white pepper and stir together. Bring the soup to the boil, skim, then reduce the heat and simmer for 50 minutes, with the lid slightly askew.

Step three Add the salt and simmer for a further 10 minutes. Before serving, taste and adjust the seasoning, if necessary. Remove and discard the bouquet garni. Pour the soup into a hot tureen and let your friends and family help themselves.

Serves 4

300g (11oz) dried butterbeans, soaked for 12 hours in plenty of cold water

20g (¾oz) unsalted butter

1 medium onion, quartered and sliced about 3mm (⅛in) thick

4 garlic cloves, sliced

4 x 100g (4oz) rashers streaky bacon, rinded and cut into 3cm (1¼in) pieces

1 bouquet garni (2 dried bay leaves and 2 fresh thyme sprigs, tied together)

200ml (7fl oz) dry white wine (optional)

1.5 litres (2½ pints) water

½ tsp salt

Watercress Soup

This soup celebrates the essence of watercress, cooking it with minimal loss of nutrients, so retaining its fresh, peppery flavour. I add ice to the watercress to halt the cooking process, so that not only the flavour but also the vivid colour is preserved. The pepperiness of watercress can vary, so taste it before cooking. If it is quite mild, leave some of the stalks attached to boost the flavour.

Step one Over a low heat, in a large pan, melt half the butter, and the onion and leek and soften for 5 minutes.

Step two Add the sliced potato and boiling water and season with 10 pinches of sea salt and 2 pinches of white pepper. Boil fast for 10 minutes, until the potato is tender, then leave to cool.

Step three Over a low heat, in a medium pan, melt the remaining butter, add the watercress and spinach, and cook for 2–3 minutes, until wilted. Add the iced water to stop the cooking, then combine with the onion, leek and potato base.

Step four Purée in a blender until very smooth, then strain through a sieve into a clean pan. Reheat gently, then taste and adjust the seasoning if necessary. Serve in a large soup tureen or individual bowls, with a swirl of crème fraîche, if liked.

Serves 4

15g (½ oz) unsalted butter

½ onion, finely chopped

1 leek, 2 outer layers removed, sliced

1 medium potato, finely sliced

800ml (1⅓ pints) boiling water

4 large bunches of watercress, stalks removed

a handful of spinach, stalks removed

700ml (1¼ pints) iced water (500ml/17fl oz water plus 250g/ 9 oz ice)

crème fraîche, to serve (optional)

Brown Chicken Stock

This recipe is cheap, the yield is good, and the stock is well flavoured, with good colour, and will not take hours of your time. Of course it is not so easy as dissolving a stock cube in water, but the results are not comparable and are well worth the effort. It is the simplest way I know to add that touch of magic to your sauces! There is no salt in the stock because it may have to be reduced before use, and this would concentrate the saltiness. It's best to add salt at the last minute. Once the stock has been made, it can be stored in small containers in the freezer to be used as and when required.

Makes 400ml (14fl oz)

100ml (3½ fl oz) non-scented oil, such as safflower, sunflower or grapeseed

1.5–2kg (3½–4½ lb) chicken wings or carcasses, finely chopped into 5cm (2in) pieces

1 onion, finely chopped

1 garlic clove, crushed

100g (4oz) mushrooms, chopped

1 tbsp tomato purée

6 black peppercorns, crushed

½ dried or fresh bay leaf

fresh thyme sprig

about 900ml (1½ pints) cold water

2 tsp arrowroot or cornflour, diluted in 50ml (2fl oz) water

Step one Preheat the oven to 230°C/450°F/gas 8. In a large flameproof roasting pan, on a high heat, brown the chicken wings in the oil for 8–10 minutes, stirring occasionally with a wooden spoon.

Step two Add the onion, garlic and mushrooms, and cook for a further 5 minutes until lightly coloured. Transfer to the oven and bake for 15 minutes until the chicken wings or carcasses and vegetables turn a rich brown.

Step three Spoon out and discard the excess fat. Stir in the tomato purée, peppercorns, bay leaf and thyme. Add 200ml (7fl oz) of the cold water, and scrape up all the caramelised juices from the bottom of the pan. Transfer the bones and liquid to a large pan, cover with the remaining cold water and bring to the boil. Skim, then simmer for 20–30 minutes.

Step four Strain the stock and skim off any fat. Whisk in the diluted arrowroot or cornflour and bring to the boil to bind the stock lightly. Set aside to cool, then chill or freeze.

Artichoke Mousse with Chervil Sauce

The quantity of artichoke in this recipe seems large. This is because much of the weight is water and will evaporate during the cooking process, leaving a wonderfully fragrant purée that gives the mousse its distinct flavour. The mousse can be cooked a day in advance, then cooled, chilled and reheated in a bain-marie.

Step one Peel and slice the Jerusalem artichokes. Steam for 20 minutes.

Step two In a liquidiser, purée the Jerusalem artichokes with the lemon juice and season to taste with sea salt and white pepper. Pour the purée into a thick-bottomed pan. Over a high heat, whisk continuously until two-thirds of the water from the purée has evaporated. You will be left with about 250g (9oz) purée. Leave to cool. Preheat the oven to 160°C/325°F/gas 3.

Step three Whisk the whole eggs and the yolks into the purée, then whisk in the cream and milk. Taste and adjust the seasoning. Brush the ramekins evenly with the softened butter and divide the purée among them. Place the ramekins in a deep roasting tin and pour in boiling water, three-quarters of the way up the sides of the dishes. Cover the ramekins loosely with greaseproof paper and bake for 35–40 minutes, until slightly convex on top with no depression in the middle.

Step four To make the chervil jus, melt half the butter in a small pan, add the shallots and sweat for 1 minute. Add the water, cream, remaining butter and chopped chervil. Bring to the boil and boil for 10 seconds, then season to taste and add a dash of lemon juice.

Step five When the mousses are cooked, pass the blade of a small knife between the mousse and the side of the ramekin and turn each mousse onto a warm plate. Spoon the sauce around the mousse, decorate with a sprig of chervil and serve.

Serves 6

special equipment

6 ramekins

1kg (2¼ lb 4oz) Jerusalem artichokes, washed

juice of 1 lemon

2 whole eggs, plus 2 egg yolks

150ml (¼ pint) whipping cream

150ml (¼ pint) whole milk

1 tsp softened butter, for greasing

fresh chervil sprigs, to garnish

for the chervil jus

20g (¾oz) butter

20g (¾oz) shallots, finely chopped

100ml (4fl oz) water

1 tbsp double cream

10g (⅓ oz) fresh chervil, stalks removed, chopped

a squeeze of lemon juice

Chicken Liver Parfait

This parfait is a bit rich, but who cares? Accompanied by a glass of red wine and a thick slice of toasted bread, it is the perfect treat to share with friends around your table. You can serve the parfait with pickles, chutney or soused vegetables.

Serves 8–10

equipment needed

a 23 x 9 x 7.5cm (9 x 3½ x 3in) terrine mould

400g (14oz) fresh chicken livers

200ml (7fl oz) milk

200ml (7fl oz) water

100ml (3½fl oz) dry Madeira

100ml (3½fl oz) ruby port

1 large shallot, finely chopped

1 tsp finely chopped fresh thyme

50ml (2fl oz) cognac

1 garlic clove, crushed

400g (14oz) unsalted butter, diced

5 eggs

toast, to serve

to cover the parfait

150g (5oz) butter, melted

Step one Check the livers carefully and cut off any trace of green. Place the livers in a large bowl, add the milk, water and 4 pinches of sea salt, and leave to soak for 6 hours. Drain well and rinse. On a high heat, in a small pan, boil the Madeira, port, shallot and thyme until reduced by half. Add the cognac and garlic, and boil for a further 10 seconds. Remove from the heat and leave to cool.

Step two Preheat the oven to 150°C/300°F/gas 2. On a low heat, melt the diced butter without letting it colour. In a blender, purée the chicken livers for 30 seconds; add the alcohol and shallot mixture and the eggs; blend for 3–4 minutes, until silky smooth. With the machine running, gradually pour in the warm melted butter. Add 10 pinches of sea salt and 4 pinches of black pepper.

Step three Strain the mixture through a fine sieve and pour it into the terrine mould. Place the terrine in a roasting tin and slide it onto the oven shelf. Cover loosely with a piece of buttered greaseproof paper and pour boiling water into the roasting tin until it reaches two-thirds of the way up the side of the terrine mould. Bake for 40–50 minutes. The top of the parfait will be slightly raised and rounded, with no dip in the centre. The inside should be 65–70°C (150–160°F); if you have a temperature probe, check this.

Step four Remove the terrine from the oven and leave to cool at room temperature for 2 hours. Then pour the melted butter over the top to prevent discoloration. Cover with clingfilm and chill for at least a day, preferably 2 days (after 2 days the depth of flavour will improve dramatically). To serve, dip the terrine mould into a roasting tin of hot water, then dip a knife blade in hot water and slide it against the sides of the terrine to loosen the parfait. Turn out onto a serving plate and serve with toast.

Bread Rolls Filled with Wild Mushrooms

The success of this dish depends on the quality and freshness of the produce. The best time for wild mushrooms is between July and October. This dish is simple to make, with marvellous, heady flavours from the forest and lots of juice soaked into a crusty French bread roll.

Step one Preheat the oven to 180°C/350°F/gas 4. Take each bread roll and slice off the top about one-third of the way down. Scoop out the soft insides. Rub the insides of the hollow and the top inside of the 'lid' with garlic, then brush the olive oil over the same surfaces. Place in the preheated oven to dry out and crisp for 10 minutes.

Step two To prepare the filling, melt the butter in a pan and add the wild mushrooms, then sauté for 1 minute. Add the water and lemon juice, and cook for a further minute, covered. Taste, and season with sea salt and black pepper, then set aside.

Step three Add the chopped herbs to the whipped cream, then taste and season. Just before serving, whisk the whipped cream into the mushrooms and their juices. Divide the mushrooms among the hollows in each bread roll, and spoon the sauce on and around. Top with the 'lids' and serve to your guests.

Serves 4

4 round, good-quality white bread rolls

2 large garlic cloves, halved

50ml (2fl oz) olive oil

for the filling

25g (1oz) unsalted butter

200g (7oz) wild mushrooms, prepared (see page 111)

50ml (2fl oz) water mixed with 1½ tsp lemon juice

1 tsp chopped fresh chervil

1 tsp chopped fresh parsley

a few tarragon leaves, blanched in boiling water for 10 seconds, then chopped

50ml (2fl oz) whipping cream, whipped

Roquefort, Walnut and Chicory Salad

Roquefort comes from the Auvergne, a region of France for which British people have a particular affection. It is a very rich cheese with a strong, spicy taste. This simple salad is one of the best ways to appreciate its flavour. Make sure the cheese is well chilled before use, so you can crumble it easily. Choose the walnuts and walnut oil carefully; if old, they will taste rancid and unpleasant. Should you wish, you can replace the chicory with any other salad leaves.

Serves 4

16 small heads of chicory

1 apple, such as Granny Smith or Braeburn

75g (3oz) Roquefort

100g (4oz) walnuts, chopped

1 celery stick, finely sliced

1 tbsp finely snipped fresh chives, to garnish

for the dressing

1 tbsp Dijon mustard

1 tbsp white wine vinegar

2 tbsp water

2 tbsp best-quality walnut oil

2 tbsp extra-virgin olive oil

Step one Cut the base off the chicory and remove any damaged outer leaves. Cut each chicory head in half lengthways and set aside. Halve the apple, remove the core and slice or dice finely. Crumble the Roquefort onto a plate and chill while you prepare the dressing.

Step two To make the dressing, whisk the mustard, vinegar and water together, then trickle in the walnut oil and olive oil, whisking constantly. Season with 2 pinches of sea salt and 2 pinches of black pepper, or to taste.

Step three Mix the dressing with the chicory, apple, walnuts, celery and two-thirds of the Roquefort. Arrange on a large serving dish or individual plates. Scatter the remaining Roquefort over the salad and top with the snipped chives.

Gruyère, Ham and Mushroom Salad with Cream and Mustard Dressing

A simple, everyday salad from my native county, Franche-Comté. Most of my English friends speed past it on their way from Paris to the south of France and in doing so bypass one of the loveliest and most hospitable areas of the country. It produces some of the very best cream and cheeses in France, which are used extensively in its cuisine.

Step one Cut the ham into strips. Slice the cheese and cut that into strips too. Cut the mushrooms into slices 3mm (1⁄8in) thick. Cut the base off the chicory and remove any damaged outer leaves. Cut each chicory head in half lengthways, then slice into 2cm (3⁄4in) chunks.

Step two To make the dressing, put the mustard in a small bowl and whisk in the cream, then the white wine vinegar. Gradually whisk in the oil and then season with 2 pinches of sea salt and 2 pinches of black pepper, or to taste.

Step three Put the chicory, both types of lettuce, ham, cheese and mushrooms in a large bowl or individual bowls, and mix with the dressing. Scatter the snipped chives on top and serve.

Serves 4

300g (11oz) smoked ham or jambon de Paris

100g (4oz) Gruyère

200g (7oz) firm, fresh button mushrooms

2 chicory heads

100g (4oz) frisée lettuce

100g (4oz) lamb's lettuce

1 tbsp snipped fresh chives, to garnish

for the dressing

1 small tbsp Dijon mustard

5 tbsp whipping cream

1 tbsp white wine vinegar

5 tbsp grapeseed oil or extra-virgin olive oil

Pâté de Campagne

Surprisingly quick and easy and a great dish to grace a dinner party. It is best prepared 2 days in advance, so the flavours have time to mature. Pickled vegetables are the best garnish, not forgetting a hunk of rustic bread.

Serves 8

special equipment

a 23 x 9 x 7.5cm (9 x 3½ x 3in) terrine mould

250g (9oz) boned pork shoulder, cut into 3cm (1¼in) dice

250g (9oz) boned belly of pork, cut into 3cm (1¼in) dice

250g (9oz) smoked streaky bacon, cut into 3cm (1¼in) dice

300g (11oz) pig's liver, cut into 3cm (1¼in) dice

1 medium egg

4 juniper berries, crushed

2 pinches of five-spice powder

½ tsp finely chopped fresh thyme leaves

50ml (2fl oz) white wine, boiled for 30–40 seconds to evaporate the alcohol

2 tbsp cognac

20g (¾oz) shelled pistachios (or almonds)

1 fresh bay leaf

2 fresh thyme sprigs

Step one Preheat the oven to 160°C/325°F/gas 3. In a food-processor, using the pulse button, chop the pork shoulder until you have a coarse mince texture, then transfer to a large mixing bowl. Repeat the process with the belly of pork, the smoked streaky bacon and the liver, combining all the meats in the bowl.

Step two Add the egg, juniper berries, five-spice powder, chopped thyme, white wine, cognac, nuts and 6 pinches of sea salt and 2 pinches of black pepper. Vigorously mix everything together with a large wooden spoon. Tip the mixture into the terrine mould and, with the edge of a spoon, press and pack the meat down into the mould. Tap the terrine a couple of times on the work surface to ensure that there are no air pockets and that the meat is compact. Press the bay leaf and thyme sprigs onto the top of the mixture.

Step three Cover loosely with a piece of buttered greaseproof paper, then place the terrine in a roasting tin and slide onto the oven shelf. Pour boiling water into the roasting tin until it reaches two-thirds of the way up the side of the terrine mould. Bake for 1 hour. The top of the pâté should be slightly rounded. The inside should be 65–70°C (150–160°F); if you have a temperature probe, check this.

Step four Remove the terrine from the oven, leave to cool at room temperature for 2 hours, then cover with clingfilm. Chill for 2 days so the flavours mature. To serve, dip a knife blade in hot water and slide it against the sides of the terrine to loosen the pâté. Turn the terrine upside down on a serving platter and tap the base to free it from its mould. Carve generous slices onto plates.

Leeks with Hazelnut and Soured Cream Dressing

The leek is often regarded as a poor relation of asparagus. In fact in France we call it the 'asparagus of the poor'. I can assure you it is as delicious as asparagus itself when served lukewarm.

Serves 4

16 medium leeks

3 litres (5¼ pints) water

65g (2½ oz) salt

200ml (7fl oz) Hazelnut and Soured Cream Dressing (see below)

Step one First be very careful about choosing the leeks, as some may have a woody core that is absolutely inedible and tasteless. Trim the base of the leek without cutting into the leek itself. Remove some of the coarser green leaves at the top. Remove the first two layers of outer leaves as these still remain stringy after cooking (they can be used for stock). Split the leek in half lengthways, running down to about 10cm (4in) from the base, and wash under running tepid water (this will remove the earth more easily). Tie the leeks in three bundles with string.

Step two Bring the water to the boil with the salt and throw in the leeks, ensuring that they are well covered with water. When the water comes back to the boil, reduce the temperature to a gentle boil and cook for 20–25 minutes.

Step three To test whether the leeks are properly cooked, slide the point of a knife right through the base of the leek. You should not be able to feel the layers. Remove the leeks from the water, and cool on a tray lined with a tea towel.

Step four Cut off the string and arrange the leeks on a serving dish. Offer the hazelnut and soured cream dressing separately.

To make Hazelnut and Sour Cream Dressing, put 1 tablespoon Dijon Mustard in a bowl with a pinch of sea salt and 2 turns of white pepper. Slowly whisk in 25ml (1 fl oz) hazelnut oil, very gradually. Add 2 tablespoons of white wine vinegar to loosen the mixture, then incorporate the remaining oil and whisk in the soured cream. Add a little water if necessary, so that the dressing coats the back of a spoon.

Smoked Haddock Fritters

The batter must be prepared at least 2 hours in advance to give it time to pr[o]

Serves 4

special equipment

an oil thermometer

8 small spring onions, trimmed

2 tbsp sesame oil

vegetable oil, for deep-frying

4 x 60g (2¼ oz) pieces of smoked haddock

Tartare Sauce (see below)

for the batter

10g (¼ oz) fresh yeast

100ml (3½ fl oz) dark beer (a stout, for instance; Guinness for the best results)

150ml (¼ pint) water

2 egg yolks, plus 3 egg whites

cayenne pepper

200g (7oz) plain flour

40g (1½ oz) unsalted butter, melted

juice of ¼ lemon

2 tbsp chopped fresh coriander

Step one To make the batter, crumble the yeast into a bowl or jug, and dissolve in the beer and water. Whisk in the egg yolks, then season with 2 pinches of cayenne pepper. Place the flour in a large bowl and mix in the yeast mixture. Whisk for a perfect mix, then stir in the melted butter. Allow to prove at room temperature for 2–2½ hours, or leave overnight in your fridge.

Step two Chop the spring onions very finely. Fry them for 1 minute maximum in the hot sesame oil, stirring constantly. Do not allow them to brown, and do not overcook. They should be al dente. Season with sea salt and white pepper, and reserve.

Step three Just before using the batter, whisk the egg whites to a delicate foam. Add the lemon juice and whisk to firm peaks. Fold in the egg whites, the chopped coriander and a pinch of sea salt.

Step four Heat the vegetable oil to 180°C (350°F) in a deep-fryer or large heavy-based pan. Dip the haddock pieces into the batter and deep-fry them in the hot fat for 2–2½ minutes until golden brown. Drain well. Divide the stir-fried spring onions among the plates, and place a hot haddock fritter on top. Serve with the tartare sauce offered separately.

To make Tartare Sauce, whisk together 2 egg yolks, 1 teaspoon of Dijon mustard, 2 pinches of salt and 3 turns of pepper. Gradually add 250ml (8fl oz) of good-quality non-scented oil, such as sunflower, safflower or grapeseed oil, in a steady trickle, whisking continuously until the oil is absorbed and the mixture turns pale yellow and thickens. Thin the mix down by adding 1 teaspoon of white wine vinegar and 2 teaspoons of lemon juice and whisk again. Stir in 30g (1¼ oz) each of chopped gherkins and washed and dried capers, 2 tablespoons each of chopped fresh parsley and fresh chervil and 2 peeled and finely chopped shallots.

Poached Asparagus with Mayonnaise

One of the truly great spring dishes. Asparagus is now available all year round but home-grown is best, and the more local the better. The UK season is very short, lasting from May until June. To help prevent the mayonnaise splitting, ensure that all the ingredients are at room temperature before you start. The reward for this simple creative act is enormous and you will never want to buy bottled mayonnaise again.

Step one Whisk together the egg yolks, mustard, salt and cayenne. Gradually, at a slow trickle, whisk in the oil. The mixture will thicken and become a rich straw yellow. This early stage is the most delicate; it is important not to add the oil too fast or the sauce might curdle. (If this happens, put another egg yolk in a clean bowl and slowly whisk in the curdled sauce. When it has all been incorporated, continue with the rest of the oil.) The more oil you add, the thicker the sauce will become. Halfway through, whisk in the lemon juice to thin it down, then continue adding the oil, more speedily now as the mayonnaise should be safe from curdling at this stage. Taste and correct the seasoning. If the mayonnaise is too thick, thin it down with about a tablespoon of warm water. Chill until required.

Step two Cut off the woody lower part of the asparagus stems. In a large pan, bring the water to a galloping boil and add the salt. Gently lower the asparagus into the rapidly boiling water, making sure that all the tips are on one side of the pan. Cover to bring the water back to the boil more quickly. Remove the lid and cook for 4–5 minutes, depending on the thickness of the asparagus; it should be bright green and tender but still a little firm.

Step three Remove the asparagus with a slotted spoon and drain on a tea towel. You can serve it warm or cold. (If you prefer it cold, plunge it into a bowl of cold water to halt the cooking process and retain the colour and texture.) Arrange the asparagus on a large dish and season lightly with sea salt and black pepper. Serve the mayonnaise separately.

Serves 4

1kg (2¼ lb) medium-sized English asparagus

3 litres (5¼ pints) water

2 tbsp salt

for the mayonnaise

2 egg yolks

1 tsp Dijon mustard

2 pinches of salt

a pinch of cayenne pepper

300ml (½ pint) groundnut oil or any good unscented oil

juice of ½ lemon

Poached Artichokes with Mustard Vinaigrette

The first artichokes of the season are imported from Provence in April but we have to wait until June or July for the English ones. Try to buy large, fat globes that feel heavy for their size, with healthy-looking leaves and no discoloration. Children love this dish, as it is so much fun to eat. You have to pull the leaves off one by one, dip them into the mustardy dressing, then scrape off the tender flesh from the base of the leaf with your teeth. When all the leaves have gone, pull out and discard the chalky bits (the choke), so you can eat the heart.

Serves 4

3 litres (5¼ pints) water

40g (1½ oz) salt

4 large globe artichokes

4 slices of lemon

for the mustard vinaigrette

1 tbsp Dijon mustard

1 tbsp white wine vinegar

5 tbsp water

a pinch of salt

a pinch of freshly ground white pepper

120ml (4fl oz) groundnut oil or any good unscented oil

1 small shallot, finely chopped

Step one In a large pan, bring the water to the boil with the salt. Meanwhile, break off the stalks from the artichokes by holding the head and twisting off the stalk: this should remove some of the tough fibres with it. Tie a lemon slice to the base of each artichoke with string – this prevents discoloration during cooking.

Step two Add the artichokes to the boiling water and bring back to a gentle simmer, with a few bubbles just breaking the surface. Place a plate over the artichokes to keep them submerged and cook for 25–30 minutes, depending on their size; the leaves should peel away easily when they are done. Turn off the heat and leave them to cool in their cooking water.

Step three While the artichokes are cooking, whisk together all the ingredients for the mustard vinaigrette in a small bowl. Taste and adjust the seasoning if required. Serve the barely warm artichokes with the mustard vinaigrette on the side.

Moules Marinière

This Normandy classic has become a worldwide favourite, yet it is one of the simplest dishes to make at home. The key, as ever, is the freshness of the mussels. A fresh mussel is shiny, tightly closed and heavy with seawater, with no 'fishy' smell. If you find mussels like this, you will be in for a feast.

Step one Wash the mussels under cold running water, but don't scrub the shells or the colour will transfer to the juices during cooking, giving them an unappetizing grey appearance. If any of the mussels float it means they are not very fresh, so discard them. Press the shells of any open mussels together with your fingers; if they don't close, discard them. Scrape off any barnacles from the mussels with a sharp knife and pull out the 'beards', then drain well.

Step two Over a medium heat, in a large pan, melt the butter then add the onion, bay leaves and thyme, and soften for 1 minute. Add the mussels and white wine, cover the pan tightly and cook for 4–5 minutes, until the mussels open.

Step three Stir in the cream and chopped parsley, then serve in a large dish or four soup plates. Give finger bowls to your guests, and lots of good French bread to mop up the wonderful juices.

Serves 4

1.75kg (4lb) best-quality mussels

15g (½oz) unsalted butter

1 onion, finely chopped

2 fresh or dried bay leaves

8 fresh thyme sprigs

100ml (3½fl oz) dry white wine

2 tbsp whipping cream

25g (1oz) fresh flat-leaf parsley, roughly chopped

French bread, to serve

Fillets of Herring with a Potato Salad

If you use large fillets, ask your fishmonger to remove the bones for you. It is essential that the fish are fresh. Fresh sardines could easily replace the herrings.

Serves 4

8 x 50g (2oz) herring fillets

for the marinade

200ml (7fl oz) water

85ml (3fl oz) white wine vinegar

½ garlic clove, peeled

caster sugar

10 button onions, peeled and thinly sliced in small rings, blanched in boiling water for 10 seconds

1 fresh thyme sprig

½ bay leaf

for the potato salad

400g (14oz) new potatoes (Pink Fir Apple or Jersey Royal), washed and not peeled

40g (1½oz) shallots, finely chopped

100ml (3½fl oz) dry white wine

50ml (2fl oz) white wine vinegar

50ml (2fl oz) groundnut oil

1 tsp chopped fresh flat-leaf parsley

Step one Score the herring fillets on the skin side about 2mm (¹⁄₁₆in) deep, and place in a small container, flesh side down. Mix together the marinade ingredients. Warm slightly in a small pan, then pour over the herring fillets. Seal with clingfilm and leave to marinate for 48 hours in the bottom of your fridge, turning occasionally.

Step two To prepare the potato salad, cook the potatoes in simmering salted water for about 8–10 minutes according to size. Make sure they are not overcooked. Strain and leave to cool until warm. Cut into 5mm (¼in) slices with the skin on.

Step three In a pan, mix the chopped shallots, wine and wine vinegar. Bring to the boil and boil for 30 seconds, then add the sliced, warm potatoes. Cover and cook for 1 minute over a low heat. Stir, then add the groundnut oil. Taste, season with sea salt and white pepper, then cool and add the parsley. To serve, place a small mound of potatoes in the middle of each plate and arrange the herring fillets on top. Spoon some of the marinating juices over with the onion rings.

Tartare of Scallops with Coriander

The scallops must be the freshest possible as they are not actually heat cooked, but served raw, lightly marinated. The tomatoes must be at room temperature so when puréed they will absorb the olive oil more easily. The scallops can be replaced by very fine slices of salmon.

Step one With the small cutter, cut out 4 x 3cm (1¼in) cylinders from four of the scallops. Cut these cylinders into six fine slices. Reserve the trimmings. Separate the scallop slices, place on a shallow tray, and sprinkle them with 1 tablespoon of the lime juice and the chopped lime leaf, if using. Cover with clingfilm and leave to marinate for 20 minutes.

Step two Chop the scallop trimmings and the other four scallops into 5mm (¼in) thick pieces. Mix in the chopped coriander with 1 teaspoon of extra-virgin olive oil and add the remaining lime juice. Season lightly with sea salt and white pepper. Place the tomato dice in a small bowl, and add ½ tablespoon of extra-virgin olive oil and the drop of wine vinegar and season.

Step three Place the steel or plastic rings on a small tray and fill up two-thirds of their height with scallop dice. Top each ring with some of the tomato dice and press a little bit with a teaspoon so that all the ingredients adhere well. Arrange five or six marinated scallop slices in a rosette shape on each tartare.

Step four To prepare the dressing, cut the tomatoes in half and remove the seeds with a teaspoon. Chop and purée the flesh in a liquidiser, adding the olive oil. Season with salt and white pepper and a pinch of sugar. Strain into a small container.

Step five Brush the top of the scallop tartares with extra-virgin olive oil, and a half turn of pepper. Slide a palette knife under each ring and lift onto the middle of a plate. Lift the ring off to free the tartare. Sprinkle a little bit of extra-virgin olive oil around the tartare and spoon the tomato dressing around it as well, and serve.

Serves 4

special equipment

a round cutter 2.5–3cm (1–1¼in) diameter

4 x 5cm (2in) stainless steel or plastic rings

8 large, very fresh scallops, shelled, trimmed and washed

25ml (1fl oz) lime juice

1 fresh lime leaf (optional), finely chopped

1 tbsp finely chopped fresh coriander leaves

extra-virgin olive oil

2 large ripe tomatoes, skinned, de-seeded and diced

a drop of white wine vinegar

for the dressing

2 very ripe tomatoes

2 tbsp olive oil

pinch of caster sugar

Marinated Red Mullet Fillets with Carrots, Orange, Coriander and Basil

It is essential that the red mullet fillets are as fresh as possible. Scoring the skin of the fillets will allow the heat to penetrate the fish, and prevent it curling. It will also allow the marinade to permeate the flesh better. When searing, the objective is to cook the fish rare. This should be done very fast in hot olive oil, then the fish should be placed immediately in the marinating container. I stipulate 24 hours for the marination, but it can be extended to 48 hours (but no longer). Scallops, sardines, herrings, fine slices of sea bream or tuna can all be marinated in the same way.

Serves 4

4 x 75–100g (3–4oz) red mullet fillets, prepared

2 tbsp extra-virgin olive oil

for the marinade

65ml (2½ fl oz) extra-virgin olive oil

100ml (3½ fl oz) freshly squeezed orange juice

juice of 1 lime

1 tsp caster sugar

6 fresh basil leaves, chopped

1 tbsp chopped fresh coriander leaves

2 fresh thyme sprigs (lemon thyme if possible)

2 medium carrots, very thinly sliced

4 shallots, very thinly sliced

Step one Your fishmonger should fillet the fish for you but you might need to remove the small bones along the middle of the fillet yourself. Run your finger along the middle to locate the bones and then remove them, using a pair of small pliers or tweezers. Pull gently so as not to damage the fillet. Score the skin lightly, with a very sharp knife about 2mm (¹⁄₁₆ in) thick so that the marinade can penetrate the flesh.

Step two In a large non-stick pan, heat the 2 tablespoons olive oil and sear both skin and flesh sides of the fillets for 5 seconds. Place the fillets on a small tray, flesh-side up. Handle gently; the fillets are very delicate.

Step three Mix together all the marinade ingredients, season with sea salt and white pepper to taste and pour over the fillets. Seal with clingfilm and marinate for 24 hours in the bottom of your fridge.

Step four Arrange the fillets of red mullet and vegetables attractively on an oval dish and serve.

Deep-fried Aubergine with Aubergine Purée

A delicious summer starter. Garnish the dish with basil leaves, if you like.

Step one Preheat the deep-frying oil to 160°C (325°F). With a very sharp knife, cut about 40 very fine aubergine slices, about 2mm ($\frac{1}{16}$ in) thick (you need 36, but allow for mistakes.). Cut the remaining aubergine in half horizontally and set aside.

Step two Deep-fry the slices of aubergine in batches for about 6 minutes, until crisp and golden. Remove from the hot oil and drain on kitchen paper. Leave to cool. Season lightly. Meanwhile, preheat the oven to 200°C/400°F/gas 6.

Step three With the blade of a knife criss-cross cuts 3mm ($\frac{1}{8}$ in) deep into the flesh side of the remaining aubergine halves. Place the aubergines on a large sheet of kitchen foil. Rub the pulp of the lemon quarter over the aubergine flesh, brush with 50ml (2fl oz) of the olive oil, season and sprinkle with sugar. Place a few rosemary leaves on each piece of aubergine, then fold the edges of the foil to make a parcel. Bake for 40 minutes until soft.

Step four Open the foil parcel and scoop the aubergine flesh into a liquidiser. Squeeze in the remaining lemon juice and add the garlic and anchovies. Blend to a fine purée, pouring in the remaining olive oil progressively. Taste and season with sea salt and black pepper.

Step five For the vinaigrette, halve the tomatoes and remove the seeds. Chop the flesh and purée finely in a food-processor, then force through a sieve into a mixing bowl, using a ladle. Season with sugar and some salt, add the vinegar then whisk in the olive oil and season with white pepper.

Step six Place 12 slices of aubergine on a tray. Cover each with a spoonful of purée, then another aubergine slice. Add another layer of purée and top with an aubergine slice. Arrange the aubergine stacks and vinaigrette on plates and sprinkle with a little olive oil.

Serves 4

special equipment
an oil thermometer

1 litre (1¾ pints) vegetable oil, for deep-frying

2 aubergines, 350–400g (12–14oz) each

for the aubergine purée
¼ lemon

150ml (¼ pint) olive oil

1 tsp caster sugar

2 tiny fresh rosemary sprigs

1 garlic clove

2 anchovies, washed briefly and patted dry

for the tomato vinaigrette
(Makes about 175g (6oz) and you will need 100ml (3½ fl oz) for this recipe)

200g (7oz) ripe tomatoes

a pinch of caster sugar

a dash of white wine vinegar

3 tbsp extra-virgin olive oil

to finish
4 tbsp extra-virgin olive oil

Comté Cheese Soufflé

I will show you here just how uncomplicated soufflés can be.

Serves 4

special equipment

4 soufflé moulds, 10cm (4in) diameter

to line the soufflé dishes

20g (¾oz) butter, unsalted, at room temperature

50g (2oz) dry breadcrumbs, plus extra for dusting

for the soufflé base

10g (⅓oz) unsalted butter

10g (⅓oz) plain flour

85ml (3fl oz) whole milk, warmed

40g (1½oz) young Comté cheese, grated

1 tsp Dijon mustard

1 egg yolk

for the soufflé mix

juice of ¼ lemon

4 egg whites

sea salt

for the sauce

150ml (¼ pint) double cream

75g (3oz) Comté cheese, grated

1 tbsp kirsch liqueur

Step one Using a pastry brush, line the four soufflé moulds with a thin, even layer of butter, and then a layer of breadcrumbs, and set aside. Pre-heat the oven to 190°C/375°F/gas 5.

Step two On a medium heat, melt the butter for the base, add the flour and whisk to a smooth consistency; cook to a blond colour. Reduce the heat; gradually add the milk, whisking to a smooth consistency. Add the cheese and mustard, continue to cook, stirring from time to time, for 3–5 minutes. Remove from the heat and allow to cool a little. Add the egg yolk and stir until the mixture is silky and smooth. Season and keep warm.

Step three Now prepare the soufflé mix. In a bowl add the lemon juice to the egg whites and whisk until very soft peaks are formed, add a pinch of salt then continue whisking until you have firm peaks. Place the warm soufflé base in a bowl and whisk in briskly one-third of the egg whites. Carefully fold in the remaining egg whites. Fill the soufflé moulds to the top and firmly tap each one on the work surface to ensure the mixture is dispersed evenly within the mould.

Step four Place the soufflés in a deep roasting tin and pour boiling water around until it reaches one-third of the way up the moulds. Transfer to the oven and cook for 7–8 minutes, then leave to cool for 3 minutes. Cover a baking sheet with a thin layer of breadcrumbs. Gently de-mould the soufflés and place on the bread-crumbed sheet. The soufflés can now stay at room temperature until you are ready to serve them to your guests.

Step five To make the sauce, bring the cream to the boil and add the cheese and some white pepper, stirring continuously. Once the cheese has melted, remove from the heat, and add a dash kirsch. Return the tray of soufflés to the oven and cook for 5–6 minutes to heat through. Serve with a dressed green salad and pour over the cheese sauce.

Assiette Albert

A small tribute to my former head gardener. The asparagus can be cooked an hour beforehand, then refreshed under cold water. The hollandaise sauce can be prepared half an hour in advance and kept warm in a bain-marie.

Step one Bring to a brisk boil in a large pan about 2 litres (3½ pints) of water. Add 40g (1½oz) salt, then throw in the asparagus. Cover until the water comes back to the boil. Remove the lid and cook for a further 5–6 minutes, according to the size of the spears. With a slotted spoon, lift the asparagus out and refresh in cold water. Drain well, then cut each spear in half.

Step two Mix the butter, chopped mint and chervil with the 100ml (3½fl oz) water in a large pan. Season with sea salt and white pepper, then bring to the boil. Throw in all the remaining vegetables – the peas, lettuce leaves and rocket if using – cover and cook for 2 minutes.

Step three Add the asparagus and reheat for 30 seconds. Place all the vegetables, plus their juices, onto a serving dish, and serve. Offer the hollandaise sauce separately.

Serves 4

400g (14oz) small English asparagus spears, peeled

20g (¾oz) unsalted butter

4 fresh peppermint leaves, finely chopped

1 tbsp finely chopped fresh chervil

100ml (3½ fl oz) water

120g (4½oz) very young peas

16 young lettuce leaves

a handful of rocket leaves (optional)

1 quantity of Hollandaise Sauce (see page 71)

Puff Pastry Tartlet with Scallops

The tartlet cases can be prepared a few days in advance and kept frozen. The tartlets plus filling can be baked an hour before serving.

Serves 4

special equipment

4 circles of silicone paper 18cm (7in) in diameter

a round pastry cutter 14cm (5½in) in diameter

250g (9oz) high-quality shop-bought puff pastry

for the filling

4 tbsp olive oil

120g (4½oz) red peppers, de-seeded and finely diced

120g (4½oz) tomatoes, skinned, de-seeded and diced

a dash of white wine vinegar

4 large scallops, roe removed

2 tbsp extra-virgin olive oil

12 fresh basil leaves or 24 fresh coriander leaves

to finish

½ tsp Dijon mustard

2 tbsp extra-virgin olive oil

Step one Lightly flour a work surface. Cut the puff pastry dough into quarters. Roll each quarter into a circle of about 18cm (7in) in diameter and about 3mm (⅛in) thickness. Place these on a lightly floured baking sheet and chill for 8–10 minutes.

Step two With the pastry cutter, stamp out four slightly smaller circles and place each of them onto the circles of silicone paper. With the pastry trimmings, prepare thin strips about 3mm (⅛in) in height and 5mm (¼in) wide. With water and a brush, moisten the outside of the circles, then curl and stick on the thin strips to make the sides of the tartlets. Chill or freeze.

Step three To cook the filling, heat half the olive oil and sear the pepper dice, then cook at a lower temperature for 3 minutes. Add the diced tomatoes and cook for a further minute. Season with sea salt and white pepper, add the dash of wine vinegar, and set aside to cool. Meanwhile, preheat the oven to 200°C/400°F/gas 6.

Step four Heat the remaining oil in a frying pan and sear the scallops for about 2 minutes. Leave to cool. When the scallops have cooled, cut them into fine slices. Place them in a bowl, and add the extra virgin olive oil and some salt and pepper. Chop the basil or coriander leaves and mix them with the scallops.

Step five Remove the tartlets from the freezer or fridge. Still on their silicone paper, place them on the baking sheet. Divide the pepper and tomato mixture among the centre of the tartlets and spread out evenly. Cover this base with the slices of scallops, making sure they overlap. Leave the sides free of filling. Transfer to the oven and bake for 10 minutes.

Step six To serve, roughly mix the Dijon mustard and olive oil together and brush over the tops and sides of each tartlet.

Risotto with Mussels

Arborio and other risotto rices have medium to long grains and a hard core, which is what produces the characteristic texture of risottos – the grains creamy on the outside while still slightly al dente in the middle.

Step one Place the mussels in a sink of cold water and pick over, discarding any that do not close when tapped with the blade of a knife. If they continue to gape, discard; they are dead. Scrape off any barnacles, using the blade of a small sharp knife, and pull away the black threads or beards. Wash thoroughly, then drain.

Step two In a large cast-iron pan, melt the butter over a low heat and sweat the 50g (2oz) chopped onion and garlic for a few minutes until soft but not brown. Add the wine, thyme and bay leaf, bring to the boil and boil for 10 seconds over a high heat. Add the mussels, cover and cook, shaking the pan, for 1 minute until the mussels are just opened. Discard any that remain closed.

Step three Drain the juices from the mussels into a small pan through a fine sieve or cloth. Pick the mussels out of their shells and keep them in their cooking juices. Bring the wine for the rice to the boil for 5 seconds, and set aside. In a separate pan, bring the water to a simmer.

Step four In a large frying pan, melt the butter and sweat the onion for the risotto for 1 minute, then add the rice and stir. Add the wine and a ladleful of hot water. On a medium heat, bring the rice to near simmering point and cook until the rice has absorbed most of the water. Add another ladle of water, stirring delicately. The rice will gradually cook as the water is added. Keep the temperature low, as on no account must the risotto boil. This process will take about 30 minutes.

Step five Mix the mussels and their juices into the risotto. Stir and cook on a medium heat for a further minute, season with sea salt and black pepper and serve.

Serves 4

for the risotto

100ml (3½ fl oz) dry white wine

1.25 litres (2¼ pints) water

40g (1½ oz) unsalted butter

80g (3¼ oz) onion, finely chopped

450g (1lb) arborio or other risotto rice

for the mussels

1.5kg (3½ lb) mussels

1 tsp unsalted butter

50g (2oz) onion, finely chopped

2 garlic cloves, roughly chopped

100ml (3½ fl oz) dry white wine

4 fresh thyme sprigs

1 fresh or dried bay leaf

Pan-fried Fillet of Sea Bream with Ratatouille

All the clean, fresh flavours of Provence can be found in this fragrant dish. The ratatouille can be prepared a day in advance and the tomato coulis a few hours in advance.

Step one Preheat the oven to 200°C/ 400°F/gas 6. To make the ratatouille, heat the oil in a large pan on a medium heat, add the onions and thyme, and soften for 3–4 minutes, without letting them colour. Add the garlic, red peppers, courgettes, aubergine, 8 pinches of salt and 4 pinches of black pepper, and cook for 2 minutes longer.

Step two Stir in the tomato purée and chopped tomatoes. Cook over a medium heat, covered, for 15–20 minutes, until the vegetables are tender. Taste and adjust the seasoning if necessary, then set aside.

Step three To make the tomato coulis, purée the cherry tomatoes with the extra-virgin olive oil, 2 pinches of salt and a pinch of pepper in a blender, or with a hand-held blender. Taste and add the sugar if necessary, then strain and set aside.

Step four Slash each sea bream fillet three times with a sharp knife (this allows the heat to penetrate more easily), and season with 4 pinches of salt and 2 of pepper. Over a high heat, in a large, ovenproof frying pan, heat the oil. Sear the fillets on the flesh side for 30–40 seconds, then turn over and cook for 2–3 minutes. Transfer to the oven and cook for 2–3 minutes longer, depending on thickness. Taste and adjust the seasoning, if necessary, then sprinkle the lemon juice over the fillets.

Step five Reheat the ratatouille and gently warm the tomato coulis, making sure it does not boil (if it did it would become grainy and lose all its freshness). Arrange the ratatouille in the middle of four soup plates and top with the sea bream fillets. Spoon the tomato coulis around and then drizzle with the best extra-virgin olive oil.

Serves 4

for the ratatouille

4 tbsp olive oil

2 onions, cut into 2cm (¾in) dice

4 fresh thyme sprigs

4 garlic cloves, crushed

2 large red peppers, de-seeded and cut into 2cm (¾in) dice

2 large courgettes, cut in half lengthways and cut into 2cm (¾in) dice

1 medium aubergine, cut in half lengthways and cut into 2cm (¾in) dice

2 tbsp tomato purée

4 plum tomatoes, chopped

for the tomato coulis

200g (7oz) very ripe cherry tomatoes

2 tbsp extra-virgin olive oil

2 pinches of sugar, if needed

for the sea bream

4 sea bream fillets

1 tbsp extra-virgin olive oil, plus extra for drizzling

juice of ½ lemon

Turbot Roasted on a Bed of Fennel

For ease, the fennel and orange can be dried up to a week in advance and stored in a sealed container. The red wine sauce can be made a day ahead.

Serves 4

for the beurre blanc

30g (1¼ oz) banana shallots, finely diced

1 tbsp white wine vinegar

20ml (¾ fl oz) dry white wine

50ml (2fl oz) cold water

120g (4½ oz) butter, cold, diced

1 tsp lemon juice

for the red wine sauce

30g (1¼ oz) butter

60g (2¼ oz) banana shallots, finely sliced

100g (4oz) button mushrooms, finely sliced

250ml (8fl oz) red wine

350ml (12fl oz) Brown Chicken Stock (see page 14)

for the turbot

20 dried sticks of fennel

4 dried strips of orange zest

6 fresh thyme sprigs

½ fresh or dried bay leaf

2 star anise

1kg (2lb) tranchon turbot

300ml (½ pint) olive oil

50ml (2fl oz) anchovy oil

Step one To make the beurre blanc, in a small heavy-bottomed pan combine the shallots, vinegar and wine and boil until you have about 1 tablespoon of syrupy liquid. Add the cold water, then whisk in the cold diced butter over a gentle heat, a little at a time, until completely amalgamated. The finished sauce will be creamy, homogeneous and a delicate lemon yellow. Enliven with a squeeze of lemon juice and season with a tiny amount of sea salt and white pepper.

Step two To make the red wine sauce, melt the butter and soften the shallots on a medium heat for 2–3 minutes. Add the mushrooms and soften for a further 2 minutes. Pour in the red wine and reduce by half. Add the stock and continue cooking to reduce by half. Taste and adjust the seasoning if required. Strain and set aside.

Step three Preheat the oven to 180°C/350°F/gas 4. To prepare the turbot, line a roasting tin with the fennel, orange, thyme, bay leaf and star anise. Lay the fish, white skin-side up, in the pan on the bed of the dried fennel mixture, and pour over the olive and anchovy oils, then season with salt and pepper. Roast the turbot for 25–30 minutes, basting frequently. Remove from the oven, cover with foil and rest for 7–8 minutes.

Step four Present the turbot along with the warm beurre blanc and red wine sauce.

Fillet of Plaice with Spring Vegetables

This dish is easy to make in your own home. There is no fish stock needed – the natural juices from the fish will create a wonderful jus.

Step one Score the plaice fillets on the outer skin side in a criss-cross pattern. Season with sea salt and white pepper. Fold the fillets in half, skin side outwards, and set aside.

Step two Preheat the oven to 200°C/400°F/gas 6. Prepare the vegetable garnish. Cook the broad beans in boiling salted water for 2 minutes. Lift out with a slotted spoon, refresh under cold water and drain. Keep the water for cooking the other vegetables. If the beans are large, peel off the skins; if they are small, leave the skins on. Set aside. Boil the peas in the same water for 1 minute, lift out with a slotted spoon, refresh in cold water and set aside. Boil the courgette slices in the water for 2 minutes. Lift out with a slotted spoon, refresh and set aside. Sieve the water. Boil the French beans in the same water for 3–4 minutes. Lift out with a slotted spoon, refresh and set aside. Boil the lettuce leaves in the same water for 30 seconds, lift out with a slotted spoon, refresh and set aside.

Step three In a sauté pan large enough to hold the fillets in one layer, melt the butter and add the shallots, then sweat for 2 minutes. Add the sliced mushrooms and sweat for a further minute. Add the wine and boil for about 1 minute before adding the water. Add the folded plaice fillets, bring the liquid to boiling point, and cover. Transfer to the oven and bake for about 5 minutes. Remove from the oven and set aside in a warm place for 3–5 minutes. This will allow the residual heat to finish cooking the fish perfectly.

Step four Lift the rested plaice fillets onto a large buttered serving dish and keep warm. Strain the juices into a medium pan, pressing on the shallots and mushrooms to extract as much liquid as possible. To finish the sauce, add the cream and whisk in the butter. Taste, adjust the seasoning and add a little lemon juice to lift the sauce. Add the chervil and chives and all the vegetables. Bring to the boil for 30 seconds, pour over the fillets of plaice and serve.

Serves 4

4 x 150g (5oz) plaice fillets

30g (1¼ oz) unsalted butter, plus extra for greasing

2 shallots, sliced

75g (3oz) button mushrooms, sliced

100ml (3½ fl oz) dry white wine

50ml (2fl oz) water

for the vegetable garnish

75g (3oz) shelled broad beans

75g (3oz) shelled young peas

1 medium courgette, sliced about 3mm (⅛ in) thick

75g (3oz) French beans, topped and tailed

8 lettuce leaves

to finish the sauce

1 tsp cream

15g (½ oz) cold, unsalted butter, diced

lemon juice

½ tbsp snipped fresh chives

½ tbsp chopped fresh chervil

Pan-fried Salmon Fillet with Sorrel Sauce

Sorrel used to grow wild in the fields of my native Franche-Comté and you can find it in the UK, too. It is very acidic and can be overwhelming, but combined with the mellow taste of salmon it works very well. Please try to buy the best salmon you can find. I am very well aware that wild or organic salmon costs a lot more than farmed salmon but it is definitely worth it.

Serves 4

for the sorrel sauce

1 shallot, finely chopped

50ml (2fl oz) dry white wine

100g (4oz) sorrel, stalks removed

100ml (3½fl oz) whipping cream

juice of ¼ lemon

1 plum tomato, de-seeded (but not skinned) and cut into 5mm (¼in) dice

for the salmon

4 x 175g (6oz) wild or organic salmon fillets, cut across from a medium-sized fish, skinned

20g (¾oz) unsalted butter

juice of ½ lemon

Step one To make the sorrel sauce, heat the shallot and white wine in a small pan on a high heat, bring to the boil and boil for 30 seconds, to evaporate the alcohol. Add the sorrel, whipping cream, lemon juice, 2 pinches of salt and 2 pinches of white pepper. Bring to the boil and cook, stirring, for 1 minute, until the cream has thickened a little. Do not be alarmed if the sorrel starts changing colour from bright green to a brownish green. This is completely normal. Add the diced tomato and set aside.

Step two Season the salmon fillets with 2 pinches of salt and 2 pinches of white pepper. On a medium heat, in a large frying pan, melt the butter until it is foaming. Add the salmon fillets and fry for 2–3 minutes on each side, depending on the thickness of the fillet. Remove from the heat and squeeze a little lemon juice over each fillet. Reheat the sorrel sauce and divide it among four serving plates. Arrange the salmon on the plates and serve immediately.

KITCHEN TABLE

Have you made this recipe? Tell us what you think at www.mykitchentable.co.uk

Pan-fried Pollock Fillet on a Purée of Potatoes with a Caper Sauce

We have fished cod to near extinction and whilst these stocks are hopefully replenishing, it is lovely to have a fish like Pollock. This fish is a little underrated; it is a member of the cod family and although not as sumptuous as cod, it is still a wonderful fish with a great texture and big flavour. This dish is part of a classic French repertoire and cooked in many homes all over France.

Serves 4

50g (2oz) unsalted butter

4 x 175g (6oz) pollock fillets, skinned and boned

2 tsp lemon juice

for the caper sauce

200ml (7fl oz) Brown Chicken Stock (see page 14)

1 fresh rosemary sprig

4 tsp small capers, washed and drained

1 tsp lemon juice

Step one Preheat the oven to 190°C/375°F/gas 5. In a non-stick ovenproof pan on medium heat, melt the butter and cook until a light golden brown colour and foaming. Fry the pollock in this for 2–3 minutes on each side to sear, until a rich golden brown. Season with a little of the lemon juice and some sea salt and black pepper. Transfer to the oven and cook for a further 5–7 minutes.

Step two Use a wide spatula to remove the fish from the pan, then cover with buttered paper and leave to rest in a warm place. The resting time will allow the fish to cook right through. The residual heat will penetrate to the centre, cooking the fish perfectly. Leave the remaining cooking juices and butter in the pan.

Step three To make the sauce, add the brown chicken stock to the juices in the pan, and boil until the sauce reaches a good consistency. Add the rosemary, simmer for 1 minute, then strain and discard the herb. Add the capers, then adjust the seasoning to taste. Lift the taste with the lemon juice. Place one portion of potato purée in the centre of each plate. Gently place the fish on top, sprinkle with a turn of black pepper and spoon the sauce around. Serve to your guests.

Roasted Monkfish with Mustard Beurre Blanc

Beurre blanc is not as daunting as it sounds. Rich in butter, it defies all the rules of nutrition but is delicious and simple to make.

Serves 4

for the herb purée

1 litre (1¾ pints) water

100g (4oz) fresh flat-leaf parsley leaves

50g (2oz) unsalted butter

1 large shallot, chopped

200g (7oz) watercress leaves

400g (14oz) spinach leaves, stalks removed

100ml (3½ fl oz) whipping cream

for the beurre blanc

½ shallot, finely sliced

2 tbsp dry white wine

1 tbsp white wine vinegar

50ml (2fl oz) water

120g (4oz) chilled unsalted butter, diced

1 heaped tsp Pommery mustard

½ tsp lemon juice

for the monkfish

4 x 175g (6oz) slices of monkfish

2 tbsp olive oil

Step one To prepare the herb purée, bring the water to the boil and add the parsley leaves. Cook for 4 minutes, until tender, then lift out the parsley with a slotted spoon and place in iced water to stop the cooking and retain the colour. Drain and set aside.

Step two On a medium heat, in a large pan, melt the butter, add the shallot and soften for 5 minutes without colouring. Turn up the heat to high, add the watercress and spinach, cover then cook for 1 minute, stirring from time to time. Remove the lid and stir for a further minute, until wilted.

Step three Add the parsley, whipping cream, 8 pinches of sea salt and a pinches of white pepper. Stir, return to the boil and remove the pan from the heat. Pour the contents of the pan into a food-processor and process for 20–30 seconds to make a coarse purée. Taste and adjust the seasoning if required. Spread the herb purée onto a baking sheet to allow it to cool down quickly. Set aside.

Step four Preheat the oven to 180°C/350°F/gas 4. To make the beurre blanc, put the shallot, wine, white wine vinegar and 1 pinch of white pepper in a pan and bring to the boil on a high heat. Let it reduce for 3–4 minutes, until almost all the liquid has evaporated. Add the water, then gradually whisk in the diced butter to create a smooth sauce. Whisk in the mustard, lemon juice and 1 pinch of salt. Taste and adjust the seasoning if necessary. Keep the beurre blanc warm by putting the pan in a bain-marie (a bowl or roasting tin of hot water) while you cook the monkfish.

Step five Pat the monkfish slices dry and season. On a medium heat, heat the olive oil and fry the monkfish slices for 5–6 minutes on each side. Place in the oven for 3–4 minutes to finish the cooking. To serve, reheat the herb purée and divide among four plates. Top with the monkfish fillet and spoon the mustard beurre blanc around.

Pan-fried Fillet of John Dory with Aubergine Tagliatelle and Tomato Vinaigrette

John Dory can be replaced by any flat white fish. Red mullet could also be used. The tomato vinaigrette and aubergine tagliatelle can be prepared a day in advance.

Step one Preheat the oven to 180°C/350°F/gas 4. First prepare the aubergine tagliatelle. Slice both ends off the aubergines. Cut them into four lengthways. Slice the flesh off the skin, leaving about 3mm (⅛ in) thickness of flesh on the skin. Cut each of these skin quarters of aubergine into strips 3 mm (⅛ in) wide to make 'tagliatelle'.

Step two Heat the olive oil for the aubergine tagliatelle in a large casserole and throw in the aubergine tagliatelle. Season with sea salt and black pepper, and add the sugar, garlic and thyme. Stir then cook over a medium heat, covered, for about 3 minutes. Add the white wine vinegar, and boil for 30 seconds. Add the water and set aside.

Step three To cook the fish, heat the oil in a non-stick pan and fry the John Dory for about 30 seconds on each side. Season and transfer to the oven and bake for 5 minutes.

Step four Remove from the oven and rest the fish for 2–3 minutes. Add a squeeze of lemon juice to each fillet. Reheat the tomato vinaigrette very briefly, whisking all the time. Reheat the aubergine tagliatelle, divide them and arrange onto each plate. Arrange the John Dory fillets on top. Spoon the tomato vinaigrette and 1 tablespoon of the extra-virgin olive oil around each plate.

Serves 4

2 tbsp olive oil

4 x 150g (3oz) John Dory fillets

lemon juice

for the aubergine tagliatelle

2 firm, ripe aubergines

50ml (2fl oz) olive oil

2 pinches of caster sugar

1 garlic clove, halved

1 fresh thyme sprig

2 tbsp white wine vinegar

2 tbsp water

to finish

1 quantity Tomato Vinaigrette (see page 45)

4 tbsp extra-virgin olive oil

Fillet of Turbot with a Red Pepper Sauce

Prepare the Provençale breadcrumbs up to 2–3 days in advance and keep in a sealed container. A good vegetable accompaniment would be Grilled Summer Vegetables (see page 148) and black olives.

Serves 4

2 tbsp olive oil

4 x 250g (9oz) turbot fillets

1 tsp Dijon mustard

for the Provençale breadcrumbs

(This makes double what you require)

100g (4oz) dried bread

1 garlic clove, crushed

1 tbsp finely chopped fresh parsley

1 tsp dried thyme

3 tbsp olive oil

for the red pepper sauce

3 red peppers

150ml (¼ pint) olive oil

50g (2oz) onions, chopped

2 garlic cloves, left whole with skin on

1 tsp white wine vinegar

100ml (3½ fl oz) water

Step one To make the breadcrumbs, place all the ingredients, except for the olive oil, in a food-processor and process to a rough, sandy texture. Transfer the crumbs to a large bowl and mix in the olive oil. Season with salt and white pepper to taste. Set aside.

Step two Preheat the oven to 180°C/350°F/gas 4. To prepare the red pepper sauce, cut the peppers in half lengthways and remove the seeds, stems and white parts. In an ovenproof sauté pan or casserole, gently heat 50ml (2fl oz) of the olive oil and sweat the onion for a couple of minutes. Add the peppers and garlic, and season with sea salt and black pepper. Cover and cook in the oven for 40 minutes.

Step three Remove the pan or casserole from the oven but leave the oven on to cook the fish. Add the wine vinegar to the pepper pan and boil on top of the stove for 10 seconds. Liquidise the peppers to a very fine purée, then trickle in the remaining olive oil. Strain the purée through a fine sieve into a small casserole. Thin down with some of the water until you get the correct texture. Taste, adjust the seasoning and set aside.

Step four In a non-stick pan, heat the olive oil until it has reached smoking point. Sear the turbot fillets for a few seconds on each side, then season with salt and black pepper. Transfer to a small casserole, cover with foil, and then cook in the oven for 7 minutes. Remove the fillets from the oven and rest in a warm place for about 5 minutes. Meanwhile, preheat the grill.

Step five Spread mustard over the top of each fillet and spoon the Provençale breadcrumbs on top. Heat and crisp under the hot grill for 1 minute. To serve, spoon the red pepper sauce into the middle of each plate and arrange a turbot fillet on top.

Poached Salmon with Hollandaise Sauce

Poaching fish in a little wine not only helps with the flavour, but the acidity of the wine also helps 'set' the protein in the flesh without using too much heat.

Step one Peel and slice the carrot and onion. Dice the celery and slice the leek. Mix these and all the remaining stock ingredients together in a large pan, and bring to the boil. Skim, then turn the heat down and simmer for 40 minutes.

Step two Prepare the hollandaise sauce. Fill a large pan two-thirds with hot water, and sit a bowl on the top edges of the pan so the base touches the water. The water should be just under simmering point. Place the egg yolks and water in the bowl and whisk vigorously over a gentle heat for about 10 minutes until you obtain a beautifully expanded, light and lemon-coloured foam, about six or seven times its original volume. Continue whisking until the foam has more texture. It is difficult to specify exactly when the sabayon is ready, but if you see small particles of cooked egg yolk this should alert you to imminent disaster. The best way to ensure success is to use a sugar thermometer – the temperature should be between 60 and 65°C (140–149°F).

Step three Pour the melted butter into the sauce, and whisk in briefly. Season with the cayenne pepper, lemon juice and a pinch of salt. Cover with buttered paper, and keep warm in a bain-marie. Prepare the spinach and watercress purée, and keep warm.

Step four Slide the salmon steaks into the barely simmering stock. Turn the heat up a little bit (but there should still be no boiling whatsoever), and cook for 5 minutes. Turn off the heat and leave the salmon steaks for a further 2–3 minutes according to thickness.

Step five Place the steaks on a tray and, with the help of a fork or knife, dig into the middle bones and lift them out carefully. Arrange the salmon steaks in a shallow dish and pour some of the stock over them. Serve to your guests, with the hollandaise sauce and spinach and watercress purée served separately.

Serves 4

special equipment
a sugar thermometer

4 x 175g (6oz) wild salmon steaks

for the vegetable stock
80g (3¼ oz) each of carrot, onion, celery and leek

1 strip of lemon zest

1 bouquet garni (2 fresh thyme sprigs, 1 parsley sprig and 2 fresh bay leaves or 1 dried, tied together)

1 garlic clove, peeled

1 tbsp salt

1 tsp black peppercorns

1.25 litres (2¼ pints) water

200ml (7fl oz) white wine

for the hollandaise sauce
3 egg yolks

4 tbsp water

50g (2oz) unsalted butter, melted

a pinch of cayenne pepper

juice of ¼ lemon

400g (14oz) Spinach and Watercress Purée (see page 123), to serve

Coq au Vin

This dish demonstrates what is truly great about French cuisine – simple, hearty food served with rustic bread to dip into the sauce.

Serves 4

1.5kg (3lb) chicken, cut into 10 pieces

1 heaped tbsp plain flour

2 tbsp olive oil

for the marinade

1 litre (1¾ pints) full-bodied red wine, such as Shiraz or Cabernet Sauvignon

3 medium carrots, cut into slanted slices 1cm (½ in) thick

2 celery sticks, cut into slices 1cm (½ in) thick

20 baby onions, peeled but left whole

1 tsp black peppercorns, crushed

1 bouquet garni (a few fresh parsley stalks, 2 bay leaves and 6 fresh thyme sprigs, tied together)

for the garnish

1 tbsp olive oil

200g (7oz) smoked streaky bacon, rind removed, diced

400g (14oz) small button mushrooms, trimmed

1 tbsp chopped fresh flat-leaf parsley

Step one Bring the red wine for the marinade to the boil, and boil until reduced by a third. Leave to cool. Mix together the carrots, celery, baby onions, peppercorns and bouquet garni. Add the chicken pieces and pour the cooled red wine over. Cover with clingfilm, chill and leave to marinate for 24 hours.

Step two Preheat the oven to 200°C/400°F/gas 6. Place a colander over a large bowl and put the chicken mixture in it to drain the marinade. Leave for a minimum of 1 hour to remove excess liquid. Reserve the liquid. Separate the chicken, vegetables and herbs, and pat dry with kitchen paper. Season the chicken with sea salt and black pepper.

Step three Sprinkle the flour on a baking sheet and cook in the oven for 8–10 minutes, until it is very lightly coloured. Set aside. Reduce the oven temperature to 150°C/300°F/gas 2. Meanwhile, on a high heat, in a large, heavy-based casserole, heat the 2 tablespoons of olive oil and colour the chicken pieces in it for 5–7 minutes on each side. With a slotted spoon, transfer the chicken to a plate and set aside. Add the drained vegetables and herbs to the casserole. Reduce the heat to medium high and cook for 5 minutes, until lightly coloured.

Step four Spoon out most of the fat from the casserole, add the flour and stir into the vegetables for a few seconds. On a medium heat, whisk in the reserved wine marinade little by little; this will create a sauce and prevent lumps forming. Bring to the boil and skim any impurities from the surface. Add the chicken pieces and return to the boil. Cover and cook in the preheated oven for 30 minutes.

Step five Heat the olive oil for the garnish in a medium non-stick frying pan over a medium heat, add the diced bacon and cook for 30 seconds. Add the mushrooms and cook for 4 minutes. Season to taste. Mix the diced bacon and mushrooms into the coq au vin. Sprinkle with the parsley and serve piping hot.

Duck Breast with Sweet Potatoes and Cherry Sauce

A great classic. The sweet acidity of the cherries complements the mellowness of the duck meat. You could use plums instead of cherries.

Step one Preheat the oven to 180°C/ 350°F/gas 4. To make the cherry sauce, boil the red wine and port in a medium pan on a high heat until reduced by half. Add the cherries, five-spice powder, cinnamon, a pinch of salt and a pinch of black pepper. Return to the boil and simmer for 2–3 minutes, then remove 20 cherries and set aside.

Step two Pour the remaining cherries and sauce into a blender and blend for 2 minutes. Strain through a fine sieve into a small pan. Add the reserved cherries to the sauce, then taste and adjust the seasoning if required.

Step three With a very sharp knife, score the skin of each duck breast six or seven times; be careful not to cut the flesh. Season the duck breasts with 2 pinches of sea salt and 2 pinches of black pepper. On a medium to low heat, in a large ovenproof frying pan, cook the duck breasts skin-side down for 10 minutes to melt the fat away and crisp the skin; spoon out excess fat two or three times. Turn the duck onto its flesh side and sear for 1 minute to seal the juices inside. Turn the duck breasts skin-side down again and place in the hot oven for 4 minutes. Remove from the oven and allow to rest for 4 minutes.

Step four While the skin of the duck is rendering, prepare the sweet potato. On a medium heat, in a large ovenproof frying pan, heat the groundnut oil and butter, and add the sweet potato slices. Colour them for 5–6 minutes on each side, seasoning with 2 pinches of sea salt and 2 pinches of black pepper. Transfer the pan to the oven for 4 minutes to finish the cooking. Serve each duck breast on a slice of roasted sweet potato, with the hot cherries and cherry sauce spooned around.

Serves 4

for the cherry sauce

50ml (2fl oz) red wine

50ml (2fl oz) ruby port

300g (11oz) fresh cherries, stoned

a pinch of five-spice powder

2 pinches of freshly ground cinnamon

for the duck

4 duck breasts, about 225g (8oz) each, off the bone

for the sweet potatoes

2 tsp groundnut oil

10g (⅓oz) unsalted butter

1 large sweet potato, about 450g (1lb), cut lengthways into slices 8mm (⅓in) thick (you will need only the 4 largest slices)

Roasted Guinea Fowl with Lentils

The guinea fowl, juice and lentils can be prepared a day ahead. The bird can then be cooked an hour in advance and kept warm wrapped in foil.

Serves 4

2 guinea fowl, each weighing 700g (1lb 9oz), trimmed weight

20g (¾oz) clarified butter

1 tbsp sunflower oil

for the lentils

20g (¾oz) unsalted butter

14 baby onions, peeled

100g (4oz) carrots, cut into 4 x 1cm (1½ x ½ in) batons

100g (4oz) smoked streaky bacon, chopped into fine strips

400g (14oz) green or brown lentils, picked over, washed and drained

a pinch of ground cloves

1 bouquet garni (4 fresh thyme sprigs and 2 bay leaves, fresh or dried, tied together)

1 garlic clove, chopped

for the juice

200ml (7fl oz) Brown Chicken Stock (see page 14), or water

2 fresh thyme sprigs

Step one Remove the wishbone and winglets from the birds, chop finely and reserve for the juice. Singe the guinea fowl over a flame to remove the feather stubs then truss the birds. Set aside.

Step two To prepare the lentils, melt the butter in a large frying pan, add the baby onions, carrot batons and bacon strips, and sweat over a medium heat for 3 or 4 minutes without colouring. Add all the other lentil ingredients, season with some black pepper, cover with water and simmer for about 35 minutes. Taste for texture and flavour, then drain, reserving juices and lentils in separate pans. Meanwhile, preheat the oven to 220°C/425°F/gas 7.

Step three In a roasting tin, sear and brown the guinea fowl in the clarified butter and oil for about 5 minutes on each thigh and 2½ minutes on each breast. Add the winglets, and season with sea salt and black pepper.

Step four Transfer to the oven and roast for 8 minutes. Remove the birds from the oven to a serving dish, wrap in foil, and rest for a minimum of 10 minutes.

Step five To prepare the juice, spoon the fat out of the roasting tin, then add the stock or water, the reserved lentil liquid and the thyme to the winglets. Bring to the boil, then simmer for 10 minutes or so. Strain, season if necessary, and keep warm.

Step six Preheat the grill. Reheat the lentils and place them on a large heatproof serving dish. Keep warm. Carve the guinea fowl and arrange the pieces on top of the lentils. Flash under the hot grill. Serve with the juice offered separately.

Pan-fried Breast of Wild Pigeon

Order the pigeons well in advance and ask the butcher to remove the skin and breast from the bone and to chop the bones and legs finely (for the sauce). Prepare the blackcurrants at least 10 hours in advance.

Step one Mix the marinade red wine and port together in a pan, and boil to reduce by half. Cool. Place the wild pigeons in a container and mix in all the ingredients for the marinade, including the reduced wine and port, and cover with clingfilm. Chill and marinate for 12–24 hours. The blackcurrants for the garnishes must be steeped in the sugar for 10–12 hours. Make the red cabbage garnish.

Step two Remove the pigeon breasts from the marinade, pat dry and set aside. Reserve the wine and aromatics as well. Cook the sugared blackcurrants on a gentle heat for 3–4 minutes. Taste, add a bit more sugar if necessary, then set aside.

Step three To prepare the sauce, in a roasting tin mix the butter and oil, and heat until rich golden in colour. Add the finely chopped carcases, and sear and colour on a medium heat for 5 minutes. Add the chopped vegetables and cook for a further 5 minutes. Spoon out the fat. Add the aromatics and the wine from the marinade, and barely cover the bones and vegetables with cold water. Transfer everything to a suitably sized pan, bring to the boil, skim and simmer for 20 minutes.

Step four Preheat the oven to 180°C/350°F/gas 4. Strain the carcases, pressing on the bones to extract as much juice as possible. On a brisk heat, reduce the stock down until there is 200ml (7fl oz) remaining. Add the blackcurrant jelly and bind the sauce with the diluted cornflour.

Step five Heat the butter in a frying pan until it foams and reaches a rich golden colour, and sear the pigeon breasts for 1 minute on each side. Then transfer to the oven and cook for 3 minutes. Season with sea salt and black pepper. Reheat the cabbage, the sauce and the blackcurrants. Cut each breast lengthways. Place a mound of cabbage in the middle of each plate and arrange the pigeon. Pour the sauce over and around, and scatter with the blackcurrants.

Serves 4

4 wild pigeon breasts
1 tbsp unsalted butter

for the marinade

400ml (14fl oz) red wine
100ml (3½fl oz) port
1 fresh thyme sprig
½ fresh or dried bay leaf
½ garlic clove, peeled
2 juniper berries, crushed

for the sauce

1 tbsp butter
1 tbsp groundnut oil
the chopped pigeon carcases
¼ onion, finely chopped
1 small carrot, finely chopped
1 tbsp blackcurrant jelly
1 tbsp cornflour or arrowroot, mixed with 1 tbsp water

for the garnishes

30g (1¼ oz, or about 20) blackcurrants, fresh or frozen
2 tbsp caster sugar
200g (7oz) Stewed Red Cabbage (see page 135)

Duck Leg Confit with Flageolet Beans

Confit is a classic dish from southwest France. Duck legs are marinated in coarse salt, which completely changes their texture and flavour, then cooked very slowly in duck fat.

Serves 4

4 large duck legs

30g (1¼ oz) rock salt

1 tbsp black peppercorns, crushed

4 garlic cloves, finely sliced

2 fresh bay leaves, sliced

4 fresh thyme sprigs, finely chopped

800g (1¾ lb) duck fat, melted

for the flageolet beans

250g (9oz) dried flageolet beans, soaked in cold water overnight

½ onion, finely sliced

4 garlic cloves, halved, plus 1 garlic clove, crushed to a purée

100g (4oz) smoked streaky bacon, rind removed, diced

2 bay leaves

4 fresh thyme sprigs

2 cloves

900ml (1½ pints) water

2 tbsp extra-virgin olive oil, plus extra to serve

a small handful of roughly chopped fresh flat-leaf parsley

Step one Lay the duck legs on a baking sheet, flesh-side upwards, and distribute the rock salt, crushed peppercorns, garlic, bay leaves and thyme evenly over. Cover with clingfilm and leave to marinate in the fridge overnight. The next day, rinse the marinade off the duck legs and pat them dry with a cloth.

Step two Preheat the oven to 140°C/275°F/gas 1. Put the duck legs in a large flameproof casserole, cover with the melted fat and, on a gentle heat, bring the fat to just below simmering point; there should be no bubbles breaking the surface. (If you have a thermometer, check the temperature, which should be 85°C/190°F.) Transfer to the oven and cook, uncovered, for about 2¼ hours, until the duck legs are very tender. Leave to cool. (You can leave the legs in their cooking fat in the fridge for 2–3 days, which will further improve their flavour.)

Step three Drain and rinse the soaked flageolet beans, then put them in a large pan with the onion, halved garlic cloves, bacon, herbs, cloves, water, 10 pinches of salt and 1 teaspoon of black pepper. Bring to the boil, skim away the impurities from the surface and then simmer on the lowest-possible heat for about 50 minutes, until the beans are tender. Taste to see if they are perfectly cooked: they should be soft and melting, not powdery.

Step four Stir the extra-virgin olive oil, parsley and crushed garlic into the cooked beans, then taste and adjust the seasoning if necessary. Take the duck legs out of their cooking fat. Over a medium heat, in a dry frying pan, crisp and colour the duck legs on the skin side for 5–7 minutes, regularly pouring away excess fat. To serve, divide the beans and some of their cooking liquid among four soup plates, top with the crispy duck legs and drizzle over a little extra-virgin olive oil.

Chicken Fricassée with Vinegar and Herbs

A little jewel of family cuisine. Try to choose an organic or free-range chicken and also a good red wine vinegar, such as a Cabernet Sauvignon. The dish can be prepared a day in advance and reheated in the oven at the temperature below.

Step one Preheat the oven to 150°C/300°F/gas 2. Heat the oil in a large casserole on a high heat, add the chicken pieces and fry for 5 minutes, until golden brown. Season with 4 pinches of salt and 2 pinches of pepper.

Step two Spoon out the fat from the casserole. Add the vinegar and butter, and boil for 10 seconds, until the vinegar has reduced. Stir to coat the chicken pieces in the reduced vinegar and butter. Add the white wine, bring to the boil for a few seconds, then add the garlic, tomato and tarragon. Cover the casserole, transfer to the oven and bake for 30 minutes (the liquid should not boil but should cook at a very low simmer, with just one or two bubbles barely breaking the surface). The chicken will be juicy and tender.

Step three To sauté the potatoes, heat the olive oil in a large frying pan on a high heat, add the diced potatoes and fry for 12–15 minutes, stirring frequently, until golden brown and tender. Season with 4 pinches of sea salt and 2 pinches of black pepper. Reduce the heat and add the butter, being careful not to let it burn. Finally stir in the parsley and shallot. Taste and adjust the seasoning if necessary.

Step four Remove the chicken from the oven. Taste and adjust the seasoning if required. Skim any fat from the surface of the cooking juices. Arrange the chicken pieces and sautéd potatoes on a large platter or 4 serving plates, and sprinkle with the roughly chopped parsley. Serve the cooking juices separately.

Serves 4

1 tbsp olive oil

4 chicken drumsticks and 4 thighs

5 tbsp good-quality red wine vinegar

15g (½ oz) unsalted butter

100ml (3½ fl oz) dry white wine

4 garlic cloves, peeled but left whole

1 ripe medium tomato, finely chopped

2 fresh tarragon sprigs, chopped

1 tbsp roughly chopped fresh flat-leaf parsley

for the sautéd potatoes

2 tbsp olive oil

4 medium potatoes, such as Desiree, Maris Piper or King Edward, peeled (if organic, leave the skin on) and cut into 2cm (¾in) dice

10g (⅓oz) unsalted butter

a small handful of roughly chopped fresh flat-leaf parsley

½ shallot, finely chopped, for garnish

Roast Breast of Mallard with Blackcurrant

Buy real wild duck, as the flavour will be much better. The legs and thighs of wild duck are often very tough, so we use them in the sauce.

Serves 4

2 mallards

30g (1¼ oz) unsalted butter

for the sauce

100ml (3½ fl oz) ruby port

300ml (10fl oz) red wine

4 tbsp groundnut oil

the chopped duck carcasses and bones

1 small carrot, diced

¼ celery stick, diced

1 piece of orange peel

2 juniper berries

200ml (7fl oz) Brown Chicken Stock (see page 14) or water

1 tsp blackcurrant jelly

1 tsp arrowroot or cornflour, mixed with 1 tbsp water

Step one Remove the breast meat from the birds and remove the wishbones. Chop the carcases, legs and thighs finely.

Step two To prepare the sauce, mix the port and red wine together in a pan and boil to reduce by half. Set aside to cool. Heat the oil in a large frying pan, and sear and colour the duck carcases and bones for about 5 minutes. Reduce the heat to medium then add the carrot and celery, and cook, stirring, for a further 5 minutes.

Step three Add the orange peel, juniper berries, brown chicken stock or water, and bring to the boil, and port and red wine reduction. Skim then simmer for 20 minutes. Meanwhile, preheat the oven to 190°C/375°F/gas 5.

Step four Strain the juices into a pan, pressing on the bones to extract as much juice as possible. Bring to the boil and reduce to about 200ml (7fl oz). Add the blackcurrant jelly, taste and adjust the seasoning adding sea salt and black pepper, if necessary. Bind the sauce with the diluted arrowroot or cornflour.

Step five In a small roasting tin just large enough to hold the duck breasts, heat the butter until it foams and turns a rich golden colour. Sear the duck on the skin side for 5 minutes, then season with sea salt and black pepper. Turn the breasts over, transfer to the oven and roast for 5 minutes.

Step six Remove the duck breasts from the oven, spoon out the fat, and leave the meat to rest, covered with foil, for 5 minutes. Carve the breasts, and season the cut sides with salt and pepper. Arrange on a warm serving dish and spoon the sauce over.

Grilled Marinated Chicken Breast with Courgette Ribbons

Although this recipe looks quite long it is very simple. It can be prepared a day in advance and then takes only a few minutes to cook.

Step one Slice each chicken breast horizontally in half, leaving it joined at one side, so you can open it up like a book. Place between two sheets of clingfilm and flatten with a meat mallet or rolling pin (be careful not to do this too forcefully or the texture of the meat will be ruined and it will taste dry). Mix together the olive oil, lemon juice, crushed garlic, thyme, rosemary and 4 pinches of black pepper to make a marinade. Put the chicken breasts in a large shallow dish, cover them with the marinade, then cover the dish with clingfilm and leave to marinate in the fridge for at least 6 hours.

Step two To prepare the marinated courgettes, mix the courgette slices with the garlic, basil, olive oil, 6 pinches of salt and 4 pinches of black pepper. Cover and leave to marinate in the fridge for at least 6 hours.

Step three To make the tomato dressing, whisk together the tomatoes, shallot, oil, water and vinegar with 4 pinches of salt. Taste and adjust the seasoning, adding the sugar if necessary. Set aside in a small pan.

Step four Season the marinated chicken breasts with 4 pinches of salt. Heat the ridged griddle pan to very hot, then cook two chicken breasts for 2 minutes on each side. Remove and set aside, and cook the remaining chicken breasts in the same way.

Step five Transfer the courgettes and their juices to a large pan. Cover and cook over a high heat for 2 minutes, until just tender. Meanwhile, gently heat the tomato dressing; don't let it boil or the flavour will be spoiled. Remove the courgettes from the pan with a slotted spoon. Put them on four plates with the chicken, spoon over the dressing and serve.

Serves 4

special equipment

a ridged griddle pan

4 boneless skinless chicken breasts

6 tbsp extra-virgin olive oil

juice of ½ lemon

2 garlic cloves, crushed

½ tsp finely chopped fresh thyme

½ tsp finely chopped fresh rosemary

for the courgettes

4 large but firm courgettes, cut lengthways into slices 3mm (⅛in) thick

½ garlic clove, crushed

8 fresh basil leaves, torn

4 tbsp extra-virgin olive oil

for the tomato dressing

4 tomatoes, de-seeded (but not skinned) and cut into 5mm (¼in) dice

1 shallot, finely chopped

8 tbsp extra-virgin olive oil

4 tbsp water

1 tsp white wine vinegar

1–2 pinches of sugar (optional)

Duck Breast with Apple, Cherry and Cinnamon Sauce

In this dish we will only need the breasts on the bone, which might make you a little unpopular if you asked for this from your butcher. So order the whole duck and use the remainder for a confit or other recipe. The sauce can be prepared a day in advance.

Serves 4

2 whole ducks

2 tbsp oil or duck fat

for the sauce

2 tsp unsalted butter

2 tsp caster sugar

1 Granny Smith apple, peeled, cored and chopped in 1cm (½ in) square pieces

100ml (3½ fl oz) full-bodied red wine

250g (9oz) cherries, fresh or frozen, stoned

100ml (3½ fl oz) water

1 x 2cm (¾ in) piece of cinnamon stick, finely ground, or a large pinch of ground cinnamon

2 cloves, ground, or a pinch of ground cloves

5 black peppercorns, crushed

a pinch of freshly grated nutmeg

for the garnish

12 whole cherries, fresh or frozen, stoned

50ml (2fl oz) full-bodied red wine

2 tsp unsalted butter

1 tsp caster sugar

Step one To prepare the sauce, melt the butter and sugar together in a pan, add the diced apple and caramelise for a few minutes. Add the red wine, bring to the boil and boil for 2 minutes. Add all the remaining ingredients and return to the boil, then simmer for 10 minutes.

Step two Liquidise the sauce until smooth, then strain through a sieve. Taste, adjust the seasoning and set aside. Preheat the oven to 200–220°C/400–425°F/gas 6–7.

Step three Chop the neck and winglets from the ducks, then remove the wishbone. Remove the thighs and legs and the backbones, leaving the breasts on the bone. Score the duck breasts lightly with a sharp knife and then colour them, skin-side down, in the oil or fat in a hot frying pan for 3–4 minutes. Roast the breasts for 8 minutes in the preheated oven. Allow to rest for 5 minutes.

Step four To prepare the garnish, place all the ingredients together in a suitable casserole, bring to the boil and simmer for 4 minutes. Remove the duck breasts from the bone. Season them on the flesh side and place each breast on a warmed plate. Spoon the sauce around and garnish with the spiced cherries.

Chicken with Morel and Sherry Sauce

This is a dish that you must cook for your friends. It is not particularly light, but who cares when it is so good! Two advantages are that it is quick and easy to make, and it can be prepared an hour in advance.

Step one To prepare the morel and sherry sauce, first soak the morels for at least 1 hour in 250ml (8fl oz) tepid water. Drain, reserving the soaking liquid, and wash the morels in plenty of cold running water to remove as much sand as possible from the little holes. Drain again, squeezing out excess water, and set aside. Strain the reserved soaking liquid through a very fine sieve or a piece of muslin to get rid of any sand and set that aside too.

Step two Season the chicken breasts with 4 pinches of sea salt and 2 pinches of black pepper. On a medium heat, in a large frying pan, heat the butter until it is foaming. Add the chicken and colour lightly for about 3 minutes on each side. Remove from the pan and set aside.

Step three On a medium heat, in the pan in which the chicken was fried, soften the morels and button mushrooms for the sauce in the remaining fat for 1–2 minutes. Season with a pinch of salt, then add the boiled sherry, 100ml (3½fl oz) of the reserved morel soaking liquid and the double cream. Bring to the boil and place the chicken back in the pan; the cream sauce must cover it. Reduce the heat to the gentlest possible simmer (with just one bubble breaking the surface) and cook for 13–15 minutes.

Step four Put the water, salt and butter for the leeks in a large pan over a high heat and bring to the boil. Add the leeks, cover and cook on full boil for 5–10 minutes, until tender. Drain well and keep warm.

Step five When the chicken is done, remove from the pan and keep warm. On full heat, boil the sauce for 6–8 minutes, until it has thickened enough to coat the back of a spoon. Reduce the heat and return the chicken to the sauce to reheat for 2 minutes. Taste and adjust the seasoning if required. Arrange the chicken and leeks on four serving plates and spoon the sauce over.

Serves 4

for the morel and sherry sauce

25g (1oz) dried morel mushrooms

250g (9oz) very firm button mushrooms, cut into quarters

120ml (4fl oz) dry sherry, boiled for 30 seconds to evaporate the alcohol

400ml (14fl oz) double cream

a pinch of salt

for the chicken

4 boneless skinless chicken breasts, weighing about 175g (6oz) each

15g (½oz) butter

for the leeks

1 litre (1¾ pints) water

10g (⅓oz) salt

10g (⅓oz) butter

2 leeks (top green part discarded and 2 outer layers removed), cut into 2cm (¾in) chunks

91

Provençale Rack of Lamb with Crushed Peas

A marvellous dish that will not take too much of your time. French-trimmed best end of lamb has had the rib bones cleaned and the chine bone cut so you can carve it easily. Ask your butcher to prepare it for you.

Serves 4

for the crushed peas

600g (1lb 5oz) fresh peas

85ml (3fl oz) extra-virgin olive oil

2 tbsp finely chopped fresh marjoram

2 tbsp finely chopped fresh mint

juice of ½ lemon

for the breadcrumbs

75g (3oz) thickly cut stale white bread

2 handfuls of very finely chopped fresh flat-leaf parsley

1 tsp very finely chopped fresh thyme

1 tsp very finely chopped fresh rosemary

4 tbsp extra-virgin olive oil

for the lamb

2 x 350g (12oz) racks of lamb, French trimmed

2 tbsp olive oil

20g (¾oz) unsalted butter

1 tbsp Dijon mustard

Step one Crush the peas in a food-processor, using the pulse button. Do not purée them; you need to retain a lot of texture. Transfer the peas to a medium-sized pan and stir in the olive oil, chopped herbs, 6 pinches of sea salt and a pinch of white pepper.

Step two Preheat the oven to 190°C/375°F/gas 5. To make the Provençal breadcrumbs, crumble the stale bread into the clean food-processor and use the pulse button again to process it to crumbs, ensuring that they have a coarse texture and are not powdery (if they are too fine, you will lose the texture). Transfer to a bowl and add the parsley, thyme and rosemary. Stir in the olive oil and season with 2 pinches of salt and a pinch of black pepper.

Step three Season the racks of lamb with 2 pinches of salt and 2 pinches of black pepper. On a medium heat, in a large ovenproof frying pan, heat the olive oil and butter. Add the lamb and colour the meat of the fillet for 3–4 minutes. Turn it onto its back (fat side) and colour for 3–4 minutes, until golden brown. Transfer to the oven and roast for 10 minutes.

Step four Remove the lamb from the oven and brush the mustard all over it, avoiding the bones. Press the racks in the Provençale breadcrumbs, so that every part is coated (this can be done 1–2 hours in advance). Return the lamb to the oven and cook for 8 minutes for medium–rare. Turn off the oven, leave the door ajar and allow the lamb to rest for 5 minutes so the meat relaxes and becomes tender.

Step five While the lamb is resting, cook the crushed peas on a medium heat, with a lid on, for 4 minutes. Stir in the lemon juice, then taste and adjust the seasoning if necessary. Carve the racks of lamb and serve with the hot crushed peas.

Calf's Liver with Persillade

Besides being very nutritious, this dish is extremely popular. There are two main keys to its success: firstly, the calf's liver must be very fresh, indicated by a pale pink colour and a firm texture, with no stickiness or smell. Secondly, it must be sliced very thinly, otherwise the texture will be completely wrong. A short cooking time is also essential. The best accompaniment for this dish is Potato Purée (see page 140). A persillade is a mixture of shallots, garlic and parsley (and sometimes tarragon), frequently used in French cooking. It is usually added to a dish towards the end.

Step one First prepare the persillade. Finely chop the parsley, shallot and garlic, and mix them together. Set aside.

Step two Pat the calf's liver dry with kitchen paper, then season the slices evenly on both sides with 4 pinches of sea salt and 2 pinches of black pepper. On a medium heat, in a large frying pan, melt the butter until foaming. Add the liver slices and cook for 1½ minutes, until golden brown underneath. Increase the heat and turn the liver over. Cook for a further 1½ minutes.

Step three With a pair of tongs, transfer the liver slices to a serving dish. Quickly add the persillade to the pan. Then add the water and lemon juice, and simmer for 10 seconds. Pour the pan juices and persillade over the calf's liver and serve immediately, with Potato Purée, if liked.

Serves 4

4 x 120g (4½ oz) slices of calf's liver, 8–10mm (⅓–½ in) thick

40g (1½ oz) unsalted butter

for the persillade

a handful of fresh flat-leaf parsley

½ medium shallot

1 garlic clove

to finish the dish

100ml (3½ fl oz) water

juice of ¼ lemon

Roast Chump of Lamb with Tomato Fondue

The success of this dish will depend very much on the quality of the lamb and on how long it has been hung. If hung properly, it will have both flavour and tenderness.

Serves 4

50g (2oz) unsalted butter

2 x 400–450g (14–16oz) chumps of lamb, well hung, boned, trimmed of all fat and tied with string to keep a tidy shape

100ml (3½ fl oz) water

6 large fresh basil leaves, finely chopped (and kept in a little water)

1 quantity Tomato Fondue (see page 144)

Step one Preheat the oven to 180°C/350°F/gas 4. In a heavy cast-iron roasting pan, just large enough to hold the two pieces of lamb, melt the butter on a medium heat. When foaming and a blond colour, sear and colour the lamb. This will take about 6–8 minutes. Season with sea salt and black pepper.

Step two Spoon out the butter, then transfer the pan to the oven and roast for 15–20 minutes.

Step three Remove from the oven and place the lamb on a plate covered with foil. Leave to rest for 10 minutes.

Step four To prepare the sauce, add the water to the roasting pan, and scrape off the caramelised juices on the bottom. Bring to the boil, then strain the juice into a small casserole. Add the basil.

Step five Heat the tomato fondue, then spoon onto the middle of each plate. On a board, cut the lamb into 1cm (½in) slices. Adjust the seasoning, then arrange the slices on top of the tomato fondue. Add the juices that the lamb has released to the prepared lamb sauce. Pour over the lamb and serve.

Pot-au-feu of Braised Pork Belly

Pot-au-feu is a French peasant dish, in which the meat, vegetables and broth are all cooked together in one pot.

Step one Place the belly of pork fat-side down and season the flesh with 3 pinches of sea salt and a pinch of black pepper. Lay the sage leaves in a line along the centre, then take the thickest part of the belly and roll it up as tightly as possible. Tie a piece of string tightly around the rolled belly; repeat this five or six times so the meat holds its shape during cooking. In order to hold the belly tightly and tie it at the same time, it is easier to have a friend helping you.

Step two On a medium heat, in a large non-stick frying pan, without oil or butter, fry the rolled pork belly for 12–15 minutes, until golden brown all over. Transfer the pork belly to a large casserole. Pour in the water, add 1 tablespoon of salt and bring to the boil over a high heat. With a ladle, skim off any impurities that rise to the surface. Reduce the heat and cook on a gentle simmer, with bubbles just breaking the surface, for 1 hour. Fast cooking would make the meat very tough.

Step three Add the carrots, garlic and bouquet garni, and cook for a further 30 minutes. Then add all the remaining ingredients except the parsley and cook for 1 hour more, until the meat and vegetables are tender. Stir in the parsley, adjust the seasoning to taste and serve directly from the pot to the table. Carve the pork in front of your guests or, if you are shy, in the privacy of your kitchen.

Serves 4

1.5kg (3lb) belly of pork, boned and skin removed (leaving a small layer of fat)

3 fresh sage leaves

3 litres (5¼ pints) water

4 carrots, peeled

6 garlic cloves, peeled but left whole

1 bouquet garni (made with 2 fresh or dried bay leaves, 6 thyme sprigs, 2 sage leaves, 1 rosemary sprig and 1 marjoram sprig, tied together)

2 celery sticks, cut into 7.5cm (3in) lengths and tied together in a bundle

4 banana shallots or ordinary shallots, peeled but left whole

2 leeks, 2 outer layers removed, cut into 7.5cm (3in) lengths and tied together in a bundle

½ Savoy cabbage, cut in 4, with the core left in to hold the leaves together

4 medium potatoes, such as Desiree, cut into quarters

a handful of fresh flat-leaf parsley, roughly chopped

Braised Shin of Veal

Wild or button mushrooms could be added to this recipe, as could green vegetables such as broccoli, green beans, spinach and so on, but they need to be cooked separately and at the last moment.

Serves 4

40g (1½ oz) unsalted butter

1 shin of veal on the bone, prepared by your butcher (knuckle sawn off the shin, and the flesh pushed along the bone)

100ml (3½ fl oz) dry white wine

400ml (14fl oz) water

2 medium carrots, each cut into 4

1 large onion, cut into 8

2 medium parsnips, each cut into 4

2 medium leeks, trimmed

2 fresh thyme sprigs

Step one Preheat the oven to 140–150°C/275–300°F/gas 1–2. In a large, oval cast-iron dish, heat the butter until it foams and turns a rich gold. Sear and colour the shin of veal on a medium heat until a rich brown, about 15 minutes. Pour off all the fat and deglaze with the white wine. Boil for 1 minute, then add half the water, all the vegetables, the thyme, and some sea salt and black pepper. Cover, transfer to the oven and cook for 3 hours. Add the remaining water halfway through the cooking time.

Step two Scatter the vegetables over a large hot serving dish. Place the shin of veal in the centre of the dish and serve the juice separately. The meat will come off the bone very easily.

Smoked Hock of Pork with Lentils

The dish can be made a day in advance and reheated. It reheats very well. The hocks must be soaked for 24 hours, and the lentils for 2 hours.

Step one Soak the hocks in cold water for 24 hours, changing the water frequently. Drain.

Step two Preheat the oven to 110°C/225°F/gas ¼. Put the soaked hocks into a large round casserole dish. Cover with fresh cold water – you may need 1–1.5 litres (1¾–2½ pints), depending on the size of the casserole. Add the bouquet garni, the vegetables, wine, garlic, peppercorns and ½ teaspoon of sea salt. Bring to the boil, then transfer to the oven and cook for 3 hours. Meanwhile, soak the lentils in cold water for 2 hours. Drain.

Step three Remove the casserole from the oven, but do not turn the oven off. Remove the hocks from the stock, and set aside in a warm place. Strain the stock from the casserole, and rinse the dish. Put the stock and the drained lentils into the rinsed-out casserole. Cover and return to the oven for 40 minutes.

Step four Add the hocks to the lentils in the casserole and reheat. Arrange the lentils in a large serving dish and place the hocks on the top. Carve and serve.

Serves 4

2 x 1kg (2¼ lb) smoked hocks of pork

1 bouquet garni (1 fresh thyme sprig, 1 fresh or dried bay leaf and 10g/⅓oz parsley stalks, tied together)

1 onion, cut in half, each half studded with 1 clove

2 large carrots, quartered, then each quarter cut in half

2 celery sticks, chopped into 2.5cm (1in) pieces

1 leek, cut into 2.5cm (1in) pieces

200ml (7fl oz) dry white wine

2 garlic cloves, peeled

½ tsp black peppercorns

250g (9oz) Puy or green lentils

Braised Lamb Neck Fillet with Butter Beans and Garlic Sausage

An excellent rustic dish from the southwest of France, home of the famous cassoulet. This dish can be prepared a day in advance.

Serves 4

4 x 300g (11oz) lamb or mutton neck fillets, sinews trimmed

25g (1oz) unsalted butter

1 tbsp olive oil

5 ripe tomatoes, cut in quarters and then in half

6 garlic cloves, peeled but left whole

1 bouquet garni (6 fresh parsley sprigs, 2 fresh or dried bay leaves, 6 fresh thyme sprigs, 1 fresh rosemary sprig, tied together)

750ml (1¼ pints) water

250g (9oz) best-quality dried butter beans, soaked overnight in cold water and then drained

100g (4oz) piece of smoked streaky bacon, rind removed, cut into 4

200g (7oz) garlic sausage, skinned and roughly chopped

chopped fresh parsley, to garnish

Step one Season the lamb or mutton with 2 pinches of salt and 2 pinches of black pepper. On a medium heat, in a large frying pan, heat the butter and olive oil until the butter begins to foam. Sear the lamb or mutton fillets for 8 minutes, turning every 2 minutes to achieve a deep golden brown colour. Transfer to a large casserole.

Step two Preheat the oven to 110°C/225°F/gas ¼. Spoon the fat from the pan and add 100ml (3½fl oz) water to it. Deglaze the pan by scraping the base with a wooden spoon to dissolve the caramelised juices. Pour these juices over the lamb or mutton fillets in the casserole. Add the tomatoes, garlic, bouquet garni and the 750ml (1¼ pints) water. Season with 4 pinches of salt and 1 pinch of black pepper. Bring to simmering point on the stove, then cover and cook in the preheated oven for 1 hour.

Step three Add the drained butterbeans, bacon and chopped garlic sausage to the casserole. Cook for a further hour, then taste and adjust the seasoning. Garnish with a little chopped parsley. Serve directly from the oven to the table.

Steak 'Maman Blanc'

For me, this is the best steak in the world, cooked the way my mother used to do it. These great women cooks understood an important basic technique: pan-frying meat in such a way that you can then create the most delectable juices with a simple medium – water. The beef can be replaced with other meat, such as veal, pork or lamb, and as long as you follow the same technique it will work just as well; however, the cooking time will be slightly longer. The best accompaniments are sautéd potatoes (see page 128) and French beans.

Step one Season the steaks with sea salt and scatter black pepper over them, pressing them firmly into the steaks on each side.

Step two On a medium heat, in a large frying pan, heat the oil and butter until the butter is foaming; it should turn light brown and smell very nutty. It is important to let it reach this stage, so that it will slowly caramelise the surface of the meat. The juices will then create deposits on the pan, which will form the base for the most marvellous pan juices. But don't let the butter burn or it will become carcinogenic, indigestible and develop an unpleasant taste. Raise the heat to medium high, lay the steaks in the foaming butter and cook for 1½–2 minutes on each side for rare, 3 minutes for medium–rare, or 4 minutes for medium. To test if it is done, press the meat gently with your forefinger. For rare, it should be soft and your finger will almost leave an imprint; medium–rare will be far more resistant and your finger will not leave an imprint; medium will feel quite firm, because the fibres will be cooked.

Step three Using tongs, transfer the steaks to a warm plate. Pour the water into the hot pan; there will be a lot of sizzling and the water and butter will create an emulsion. Scrape the base of the pan with a wooden spoon to release the caramelised residue, which will give taste and colour to this succulent juice. Pour the juice onto the steaks and serve immediately.

Serves 4

4 x 225g (8oz) rump or sirloin steaks about 2cm (¾in) thick, fat trimmed

2 tbsp olive oil

65g (2½ oz) unsalted butter

200ml (7fl oz) water

Roast Rib of Beef

You could serve a very delicious red wine sauce with the meat. Sweat 4 finely chopped shallots in butter for 2 minutes, add 500ml (17fl oz) red wine and reduce down to 200ml (7fl oz). Add this to the roasting pan instead of the water. Boil, then strain and whisk in 30g (1¼oz) unsalted butter. Season with salt and pepper.

Serves 4

100g (4oz) beef dripping

1 x 1.75kg (4lb) rib of mature beef (2 rib bones), well hung

500g (18oz) beef or veal trimmings

2 garlic cloves, in their skins

300ml (½ pint) water

Step one Preheat the oven to 150°C/300°F/gas 2. Heat the beef dripping in a roasting tin and brown both the meat and the beef or veal trimmings for about 7–10 minutes.

Step two Season the joint with sea salt and black pepper, and arrange it on the trimmings. Add the garlic cloves to the tin. Transfer to the oven and roast for 2 hours, basting from time to time.

Step three Remove the joint from the oven, and remove it from the tin. Season with salt and pepper, and wrap in foil. Rest for 20–30 minutes in a warm place, above the oven, for instance.

Step four Meanwhile, make the juice. Spoon most of the fat from the roasting tin. Add the water to the juices left in it. Bring to the boil and scrape and stir the caramelised juices stuck on the bottom of the pan to create a delicious juice. Taste, adjust the seasoning, then strain and set aside until ready to serve. When rested, the meat can be carved in front of your guests or in the privacy of your kitchen.

Pan-fried Lamb Sweetbreads with a Fricassée of Wild Mushrooms

Other vegetables can be added to the wild mushrooms, such as peas, French beans, button mushrooms, young spinach leaves, diced tomatoes. Other herbs can be added, such as basil, tarragon or chervil.

Step one Soak the sweetbreads in cold water overnight, or thoroughly rinse under cold running water, to remove any traces of blood. Blanch the sweetbreads in plenty of boiling water for 10 seconds. With a slotted spoon, remove and refresh in cold water. Drain, pat dry and, with a small knife, carefully peel off and discard the membrane around each sweetbread. Reserve on a tea towel.

Step two Scrape the cups and stalks of the wild mushrooms very gently with a small paring knife and cut off the base of the stalks. Wash them very briefly in plenty of water. Pat them dry, then quarter or halve according to size, and set aside.

Step three Over a medium heat, melt 2 tablespoons of the butter in a non-stick pan until it foams and becomes a rich gold. Add the sweetbreads and colour them for about 5 minutes on each side. Spoon out the fat, then season the sweetbreads with sea salt and white pepper. Keep warm, covered, and set aside.

Step four Sweat the shallots in the remaining butter for 1 minute without colouring. Add the wild mushrooms, increase the heat, and cook for 2 minutes. Season with salt and white pepper.

Step five To finish the sauce, add the lemon juice and water to the mushrooms, and bring to the boil. Add the cream, then whisk in the cold diced butter. Taste and adjust the seasoning. Add the parsley and chives. Serve five sweetbreads in the middle of each plate or dish, and spoon the wild mushrooms and the sauce around.

Serves 4

20 lamb sweetbreads (from the heart)

300g (11oz) wild mushrooms such as girolles (or button mushrooms)

3 tbsp unsalted butter

2 shallots, finely chopped

to finish the sauce

1 tsp lemon juice

50ml (2fl oz) water

1 tbsp whipping cream

20g (¾oz) cold unsalted butter, diced

1 heaped tbsp finely chopped fresh parsley

½ tbsp finely snipped fresh chives

Braised Venison with a Chocolate Sauce

This dish actually gains from being cooked 24 hours in advance, then being reheated at the same temperature for about 30 minutes. Serve garnished with Braised Chestnuts (see page 143), if you like.

Serves 4

4 x 250g (9oz) pieces of venison shoulder

50ml (2fl oz) sunflower oil

sea salt and freshly ground black pepper

for the marinade

1 bottle (750 ml/ 1¼ pints) red wine

8 juniper berries, crushed

12 black peppercorns, crushed

2 bay leaves

1 fresh thyme sprig

1 strip of orange peel

1 medium carrot, diced

1 large onion, chopped

4 garlic cloves, peeled

1 celery stick, chopped

for the sauce

1 tbsp tomato purée

350–400ml (12–14fl oz) water

1 tbsp redcurrant jelly

30g (1¼ oz) dark chocolate, grated

Step one To marinate the venison, put the red wine in a pan and boil to reduce by one-third. Allow to cool down to room temperature. Place the venison in a large container and cover with the reduced wine and all the remaining marinade ingredients. Chill and allow to marinate for 24 hours.

Step two Preheat the oven to 110°C/225°F/gas ¼. Drain the venison and the vegetables, and pat them dry. Reserve the wine. In a non-stick pan, heat the sunflower oil until smoking and sear and colour both pieces of venison on all sides to a good deep brown. This will take about 10 minutes. Transfer the venison pieces to a cast-iron casserole.

Step three In the oil remaining in the non-stick pan, colour the drained vegetables and seasonings lightly, about 5 minutes, then transfer them to the casserole with the venison. To make the sauce, add the tomato purée to the non-stick pan and cook for 1–2 minutes. Add the reserved red wine from the marinade, and bring to the boil. Pour over the venison, vegetables and seasonings in the casserole, and barely cover with the water. Season lightly with sea salt. Bring to the boil for 1 minute, skim, then cover with a tight lid. Transfer to the oven and cook for 3½ hours.

Step four To finish the sauce, strain the juices into a large pan and reduce on full heat to about 300ml (½ pint). Reduce the heat until the sauce barely simmers, then add the redcurrant jelly. Adjust the seasoning adding sea salt and black pepper, if necessary, and whisk in the grated chocolate. Mix the venison and vegetables back into the sauce, and reheat gently. Add the chestnuts if using. You may serve the venison from the casserole or transfer it to a nice serving dish.

Roasted Pork Fillet with Onion and Garlic Purée

This dish can be prepared with veal fillets instead, if you like.

Step one Preheat the oven to 180°C/350°F/gas 4. On a medium heat, in a small roasting tin, heat the butter until it foams. Sear and colour the fillets and the spare ribs on all sides for approximately 10 minutes until both fillets and bones are beautifully caramelised to a golden brown.

Step two Add the garlic and thyme, season with sea salt and black pepper, transfer to the oven and roast for 5–7 minutes.

Step three Spoon out the fat. Remove the fillets and ribs, season them again, and keep warm, covered with foil. To make the sauce, place the roasting tin on a medium heat, add the water and bring to the boil. Scrape the bottom of the pan to dilute all the caramelised juices. Simmer for 5 minutes. Strain into a casserole. On full heat, reduce the liquid for 5 minutes, until you have about 150ml (¼ pint). Taste and adjust the seasoning.

Step four Heat the onion and garlic purée. Pour the liquid the fillets and ribs will have released while resting into the sauce and heat the sauce through. Discard the ribs and reheat the fillets in the oven for 2 minutes, if necessary. Carve into thin slices and arrange in a warm serving dish. Pour the sauce over and serve with the onion and garlic purée offered separately. Alternatively, spread the onion and garlic purée on the middle of each plate, and fan the fillet slices over. Serve the sauce separately.

Serves 4

50g (2oz) unsalted butter

2 x 400g (14oz) pork fillets, trimmed of all sinews

300g (11oz) pork spare ribs, finely chopped

1 garlic clove, chopped

1 fresh thyme sprig

200ml (7fl oz) water

to serve

Onion and Garlic Purée (see page 131)

Fillet of Beef with Basil Sauce and Deep-fried Capers

Both the sauce and the Black Olive Purée can be made a day or two ahead. The capers can be deep-fried 2–3 hours in advance and kept on kitchen paper. Serve with Sautéd New Potatoes with Spring Onions (page 147).

Serves 4

20g (¾oz) unsalted butter

4 x 150g (5oz) fillets matured beef (pure Aberdeen Angus if possible), or 4x175g (6oz) rump steaks

for the basil sauce

40g (1½oz) Dijon mustard

100ml (3½fl oz) extra-virgin olive oil

20g (¾oz) pickled capers, rinsed and patted dry

60g (2¼oz) fresh basil leaves with stalks, roughly chopped

2 garlic cloves, chopped

for the garnishes

500ml (17fl oz) vegetable oil, for deep-frying

32 pickled capers, rinsed and patted dry

Step one Preheat the oven to 200°C/400°F/gas 6. The ingredients for the basil sauce will make 200ml (7fl oz) of sauce. For this recipe you need only half of that, so keep the remainder in a small jar in the fridge. Added to pasta, it will be absolutely delicious. To make the basil sauce, place the mustard in a small mixing bowl and slowly whisk in the olive oil until well incorporated. Spoon the mixture into a liquidiser, add all the remaining sauce ingredients and purée finely. Season to taste with 2 pinches each of sea salt and black pepper. Pour into a small container.

Step two To prepare the garnishes, heat the oil until it smokes lightly. Deep-fry the capers in a frying basket for 30 seconds, then drain well on kitchen paper. Place the olive purée in a small casserole.

Step three Melt the butter in a roasting tin until foaming, then pan-fry the steaks for 1 minute on each side until well coloured. Season with salt and pepper, transfer to the oven and roast for 5 minutes (rare) or 8 minutes (medium-rare). Adjust the seasoning and leave to rest in a warm place for 2–3 minutes, loosely covered with foil.

Step four Place half the basil sauce (reserving the other half to use another time) in a small casserole, and heat it up for a few minutes, stirring. Do the same with the olive purée. (Or heat both through in the oven for about 10 minutes.) Arrange the steaks on a flat serving dish and spoon the basil sauce over them, along with any escaped meat juices. Add one little turn of ground pepper, garnish with the capers and serve.

Petits Pois à la Française

Freshly picked young peas are always the best but frozen peas are excellent, too. If you prefer, you could omit the bacon and stir in some parsley and chervil at the end instead to create a delicious vegetarian alternative.

Step one On a low heat, in a small pan, melt the butter, add the baby onions and bacon lardons, and soften for 2–3 minutes, without colouring.

Step two Add the water, sugar, 5 pinches of salt and a pinch of black pepper, and bring to the boil. Cover and reduce the heat to just below a simmer (with bubbles just breaking the surface). Cook for 15–20 minutes, until the onions are translucent, soft and melting but still retain some texture.

Step three Remove the lid, turn the heat to high and add the peas and lettuce leaves. Stir, then cover and cook for 1–2 minutes, until the peas are tender. Taste and adjust the seasoning if required.

Serves 4

25g (1oz) unsalted butter

20 baby onions, peeled

50g (2oz) smoked streaky bacon, rind removed, cut into lardons (little strips) 3mm (⅛in) thick

200ml (7fl oz) water

3 pinches of sugar

400g (14oz) shelled young fresh peas or frozen peas

1 Webbs lettuce or other soft lettuce, leaves separated

Cabbage with Smoked Bacon and Caraway Seeds

Personally, I prefer to blanch the cabbage to remove some of its very powerful taste. It is always better to buy bacon that is in the piece rather than the already pre-cut slices; or get your butcher to slice the bacon in front of you. Newly sliced bacon will have a much better taste and texture.

Serves 4

1 Savoy cabbage

1 tbsp unsalted butter

150g (5oz) smoked streaky bacon, cut into fine strips

2 tsp caraway seeds, crushed

Step one To prepare the cabbage, cut off its stem and remove the coarse outer leaves. Halve the cabbage, cut out the cores and chop each half finely into 3mm (⅛in) thick slices. Wash in plenty of water, drain well and reserve.

Step two Bring 2 litres (3½ pints) of water to a full boil with 30g (1¼oz) of salt, and boil the shredded cabbage for 5 minutes. Refresh in cold water, drain and reserve.

Step three In a large cast-iron pan, melt the butter and sweat the bacon for 2 minutes. Add the cabbage and crushed caraway seeds, and mix well. Cover and cook for a further 5 minutes. Taste and adjust the seasoning, and serve.

Spinach and Watercress Purée

If you do not serve the purée straight away, cool it down on ice so that it retains both colour and flavour. Reheat at a later stage.

Step one In a large pan heat the butter until it starts to foam. Add the spinach and watercress, ½ teaspoon of sea salt and a pinch of black pepper, and cook for 3 minutes, covered.

Step two Pour the mixture into the liquidiser, add the cream, if using, and mix for about 10 seconds to a rough texture. Place in a warm serving dish and serve.

Serves 4

20g (¾oz) unsalted butter

300g (11oz) spinach leaves, washed, drained and tough stalks removed

200g (7oz) watercress, washed, drained and leaves picked from the stalks

100ml (3½fl oz) whipping cream (optional)

Celeriac Purée

This purée goes particularly well with game and roast meats. Parsnips can be puréed in the same way, but replace the milk with water.

Serves 4

500g (18oz) celeriac, peeled

500ml (17fl oz) milk

50ml (2fl oz) double cream

30g (1¼ oz) unsalted butter

lemon juice

Step one Chop the celeriac roughly into 1cm (½in) cubes. Heat the milk and simmer the celeriac cubes in it for 15–20 minutes until tender.

Step two Strain the celeriac and purée in a food-processor. Stir the cream and butter into the purée, then season with sea salt and black pepper. Add a dash of lemon juice and serve.

French Beans in Butter

Swiss chard leaves can be cooked in this way as well. And you can cook broccoli florets like this too, for 6–8 minutes, according to size; similarly with asparagus stalks.

Step one Bring 1.5 litres (2½ pints) of water to the boil with the salt. Cook the beans, uncovered, for 3–3½ minutes, according to size. Taste, and if ready, drain and plunge them into cold water for 5 minutes, to arrest the cooking process, then drain again. Reserve.

Step two To finish the dish, heat the butter and the 2 tablespoons of water together to emulsify. Mix in the beans, season with salt and black pepper, and cook for 1 minute, then serve.

Serves 4

25g (1oz) salt

400g (14oz) French beans, topped and tailed

40g (1½oz) butter

2 tbsp water

Sautéd Potatoes

The possible additions to this recipe are endless – why not try bacon, ham, tomatoes, eggs or cheese and so on?

Serves 4

550g (1¼ lb) potatoes (use Desiree, King Edward, Cara or Maris Piper)

2 tbsp corn or sunflower oil

2 tbsp unsalted butter

1 shallot, peeled and finely chopped (optional)

20g (¾ oz) chopped fresh parsley mixed with ½ garlic clove, peeled and puréed (optional)

Step one Wash and peel the potatoes, and dice into 1cm (½in) cubes. Wash again in plenty of cold water. Drain well and pat dry with a cloth.

Step two In a large non-stick frying pan heat the oil to very hot, then fry the potatoes on a medium-to-high heat, turning them from time to time, for 8 minutes.

Step three Spoon out the oil, add the butter and the finely chopped shallot, if using, and cook for a further 2 minutes. Season with sea salt and black pepper, stir in the parsley and garlic mix, if using, and serve.

Have you made this recipe? Tell us what you think at
www.mykitchentable.co.uk/blog

KITCHEN
TABLE

Onion and Garlic Purée

This purée goes particularly well with lamb or any Provençale dish.

Step one Cut the garlic in half lengthways, and remove and discard the central green germ, which is bitter. Simmer the garlic in 1 litre (1¾ pints) of water for 12–15 minutes. Drain well and reserve.

Step two In a covered cast-iron pan, over a gentle heat, heat the olive oil and sweat the onion for about 15–20 minutes. Do not colour. Stir from time to time.

Step three Add the simmered garlic to the onion, along with the thyme and cream, and cook for a further 10 minutes. Leave to cool.

Step four Remove the thyme, then liquidise the onion mixture to a purée. Enrich with the extra-virgin olive oil, season to taste wtih sea salt and white pepper, and serve.

Serves 4

12 large garlic cloves

50ml (2fl oz) olive oil

700g (1lb 6oz) onions, or 2 large onions, chopped

4 fresh thyme sprigs

100ml (3½ fl oz) double cream

50ml (2fl oz) extra-virgin olive oil

Gratin Dauphinois

Seriously satisfying – layers of potato cooked in a rich garlic cream with Gruyère cheese. This dish goes best with roast meat, particularly beef. The potato variety is important. I find that Desiree and Belle de Fontenay work best, and both are usually available in supermarkets. The gratin can be cooked an hour or so before the meal and then reheated 20 minutes before serving.

Serves 4

special equipment

a 20cm (8in) gratin dish

4 medium potatoes (Desiree or Belle de Fontenay), weighing about 450g (1lb) in total

300ml (½ pint) full-fat milk

100ml (3½ fl oz) double cream

8 gratings of nutmeg

100g (4oz) Gruyère, grated

½ garlic clove

Step one Preheat the oven to 120°C/250°F/gas ½ then peel the potatoes and slice them 2mm (1/16 in) thick – a mandoline will make the job easier. Do not wash the potato slices, as you need to keep the starch in them to help thicken the cream.

Step two On a medium heat, in a medium pan, bring the milk and cream to the boil. Add the sliced potatoes and stir to coat them with the cream. Season with the nutmeg, 5 pinches of salt and 2 pinches of black pepper. Reduce the heat and simmer for 8–10 minutes, stirring every 2 minutes to prevent the mixture sticking to the base of the pan and to distribute the heat throughout the potatoes. Stir in the grated cheese and then remove the pan from the heat.

Step three Rub the gratin dish with the garlic. With a spatula, spread the potato mixture out evenly in the dish. Bake for 35 minutes; there should be tiny bubbles on the surface of the dish. The gratin is cooked when the tip of a sharp knife cuts into it with little resistance (you shouldn't feel the layers).

Step four To brown the top, place the gratin under a hot grill for 2–3 minutes. Leave to rest for 5 minutes before serving.

Stewed Red Cabbage

This side dish goes very well with Pan-fried Breast of Pigeon on page 79.

Step one Cut the cabbage in half and remove the central cores. Remove any torn or bruised outer leaves. Chop each half finely into 3mm (⅛in) thick slices.

Step two In a cast-iron pan, melt the butter and sweat the shredded cabbage for about 10 minutes, stirring from time to time. Add the red wine, and simmer to reduce by half. Add the ruby port, blackcurrant jelly and some sea salt and black pepper. Cover and cook on a very slow heat for a further 2 hours. Taste and adjust the seasoning, adding a little bit of sugar if necessary, and serve.

Serves 4

500g (18oz) red cabbage

60g (2¼ oz) unsalted butter

100ml (3½ fl oz) red wine

200ml (7fl oz) ruby port

2 tbsp blackcurrant jelly

caster sugar (optional)

Pancake Potatoes

Very finely chopped ham, pan-fried smoked bacon strips or chives would be pleasant additions.

Serves 4

500g (18oz) potatoes, peeled and quartered (use Desiree, King Edward, Cara or Maris Piper)

4 eggs, lightly beaten

50g (2oz) plain flour, sifted

100ml (3½ fl oz) milk

100ml (3½ fl oz) double cream

freshly grated nutmeg

50g (2oz) unsalted butter

Step one Cover the potatoes with salted water and bring to the boil, then simmer for 20 minutes.

Step two Drain the potatoes well, then pass them through a potato ricer into a casserole dish and leave to cool slightly. Add the eggs, stirring all the time, then the flour, milk and cream. Season with grated nutmeg and some sea salt and white pepper.

Step three Melt the butter in a large non-stick pan on a medium heat until it becomes rich gold in colour and foamy. Using a dessertspoon, gently spoon five or six little potato mixture pancakes into the pan; these will shape themselves. Cook for 1 minute on each side, turning them with a palette knife. Drain and serve.

Braised Fennel with Cardamom

This can be made 1–2 days in advance and kept in the fridge. The fennel can be served whole, as a vegetable, but it can also be puréed, to serve as a vegetable purée (good with lamb) or as a sauce (good with red mullet).

Step one Preheat the oven to 180°C/350°F/gas 4. In a flameproof casserole heat the oil and sweat the fennel for about 10 minutes. Do not colour.

Step two Add the garlic, thyme, black olives, cardamom and water, and season with sea salt and white pepper. Bring to the boil, cover, transfer to the oven and cook for 1½–2 hours. Serve.

Serves 4

50ml (2fl oz) extra-virgin olive oil

500g (18oz) baby fennel bulbs, or large bulbs cut into 4–6 pieces, according to size

2 garlic cloves, sliced

2 fresh thyme sprigs

4 black olives, stoned

3 cardamom pods, lightly crushed

500ml (17fl oz) water

Potato Purée

A French potato purée is so different from an English mash. One is light, with fluffy peaks, melting and completely delicious; the other is dense and heavy, folds in your stomach, and has only one purpose – to fill you up … The variety of potato used is of the utmost importance, since it will define the taste, texture and lightness of the purée. The best potatoes to use are Desiree, Belle de Fontenay, Estima or Maris Piper. The potential variations on this dish are enormous – try adding garlic, olive oil, mustard or nutmeg, and any herbs you like.

Serves 4

1kg (2¼ lb) Desiree, Belle de Fontenay, Estima or Maris Piper potatoes, peeled and cut into quarters

2 litres (3½ pints) cold water

20g (¾oz) salt

to finish the purée

175–200ml (6–7fl oz) full-fat milk, boiled

75g (3oz) unsalted butter, melted

Step one Put the potatoes, water and salt in a large pan and bring to the boil on a high heat. Reduce the heat so that the water is gently simmering (with bubbles just breaking the surface) and cook for 25–30 minutes, until the potatoes are soft. Do not let it boil rapidly or the potatoes will be overcooked and watery.

Step two Strain the cooked potatoes through a colander and leave for 2–3 minutes to let the excess steam escape. Pass the potatoes through a potato ricer or sieve, or mash them thoroughly with a potato masher.

Step three Return the potato purée to the pan and gradually mix in the hot milk (reserve a little). Then stir in the melted butter and season with 2 pinches of salt and 2 pinches of white pepper. Taste and adjust the seasoning if necessary. If the purée is too firm, thin it down with the remaining milk. You have the perfect purée when it is fluffy, forms firm peaks and melts in your mouth.

Braised Chestnuts

These chestnuts are delicious with Braised Venison (see page 112). It is important to score all the way round the chestnuts before boiling them. This allows the boiling water to react and soften both the skins, so that they can be easily removed.

Step one With a small knife, make an incision through the skin around each chestnut. Bring to the boil 2 litres (3½ pints) of water, add the chestnuts and cook for 30 seconds. Drain in a colander and remove both the hard outer shell and the thin inner skin.

Step two Sweat the onion and celery in the butter in a medium-sized pan for a few minutes. Add the shelled chestnuts and cover with water (about 300ml/½ pint). Add the lemon juice, sugar, salt and some white pepper, cover with a lid, and cook at just under simmering point for 20 minutes.

Step three Drain off and discard any liquid, and serve the chestnuts in a warmed serving bowl.

Serves 4

500g (18oz) fresh chestnuts

¼ onion, peeled and chopped

1 celery stick, chopped

20g (¾oz) unsalted butter

juice of ¼ lemon

1 heaped tsp caster sugar

1 tsp salt

Tomato Fondue

These tomatoes are 'stewed' to an intense red paste. This garnish dish can be made a day in advance.

Serves 4

50ml (2fl oz) olive oil

½ medium onion, finely chopped

1 tbsp tomato purée

500g (18oz) Roma tomatoes, de-seeded and finely chopped (for a more refined stew, first blanch the tomatoes in boiling water for 10 seconds and peel off the skin)

2 fresh thyme sprigs

1 fresh or dried bay leaf

2 garlic cloves, crushed

1 tsp caster sugar

100ml (3½ fl oz) extra-virgin olive oil

Step one Preheat the oven to 200°C/400°F/gas 6. In a roasting tin on top of the stove, heat the oil and sweat the onion for 8–10 minutes. Do not colour.

Step two Add the tomato purée and cook for a further 5 minutes. Add the chopped tomatoes, thyme, bay leaf, garlic, sugar, and some sea salt and black pepper. Bring to the boil, the transfer to the oven and cook, uncovered, for 20 minutes, stirring from time to time.

Step three Place the tomato fondue in a casserole and whisk in the extra-virgin oil to enrich it. Make sure the fondue is smooth and amalgamated. Set aside to cool and then chill or grind over some black pepper and serve immediately.

Sautéd New Potatoes with Spring Onions

This recipe would make a good accompaniment to Fillet of Beef with Basil Sauce and Deep-fried Capers on page 116.

Step one Slice the potatoes into 5mm (¼in) rounds. Heat the oil in a large non-stick pan and sauté the potatoes for about 5 minutes.

Step two Spoon out the oil and add the butter. Cook for a further 10 minutes until the potatoes have reached a golden brown colour, stirring continuously. Halfway through the cooking time, mix in the finely chopped spring onions. Season with sea salt and black pepper, and serve.

Serves 4

500g (18oz) new potatoes, washed but not peeled

50ml (2fl oz) sunflower oil

2 tbsp unsalted butter

8 spring onions, very finely chopped

Grilled Summer Vegetables

Vegetables such as lettuce, chicory and fennel grill very well, but need to be blanched first in boiling water for 30–60 seconds.

Serves 4

special equipment

a ridged cast-iron grill pan

2 courgettes, cut lengthways into 3mm (⅛in) slices

1 aubergine, cut widthways into 5mm (¼in) slices

1 red pepper, skinned, halved and de-seeded, each half cut in two

2 tomatoes, skinned, halved and de-seeded

2 tbsp balsamic vinegar

for the marinade

100ml (3½ fl oz) extra-virgin olive oil

2 garlic cloves, sliced

4 fresh thyme sprigs, or a large pinch of dried thyme

6 fresh basil leaves

Step one First mix together the ingredients for the marinade, then mix in all the prepared vegetables so that they are all coated with the olive oil. Cover with clingfilm and marinate at room temperature for 6–12 hours.

Step two Brush the ridged grill pan with the marinade, place on a medium heat and grill the courgettes and tomatoes for 2 minutes on each side. Then grill the aubergines and peppers for 4 minutes on each side. Season with sea salt and black pepper, place the vegetables onto a serving dish and sprinkle with the balsamic vinegar.

Carrots with Parsley

Serve this recipe with Calf's Liver with Persillade on page 95 along with Potato Purée on page 140.

Step one Melt the butter in a pan and sweat the shallot in this for 2–3 minutes. Add the carrots and stir so that they are all coated in the butter. Add the garlic and water, cover and cook for 15–20 minutes over a gentle heat.

Step two Season the carrots with sea salt and white pepper. Add the chopped parsley and the cream, if using, and cook for a further 3 minutes. Serve.

Serves 4

1½ tbsp unsalted butter

2 shallots, finely chopped

4 large carrots, sliced about 3mm (⅛in) thick

½ garlic clove, crushed

100ml (3½ fl oz) water

2 tbsp finely chopped fresh parsley

100ml (3½ fl oz) whipping cream (optional)

Stuffed Tomatoes

For this dish you need proper Marmande tomatoes, grown outdoors.

Serves 4

4 large, ripe Marmande or beef tomatoes, about 200g (7oz) each

1 tbsp extra-virgin olive oil

snipped fresh chives, to garnish

for the tomato sauce

3 tbsp olive oil

1 medium onion, chopped

2 garlic cloves, crushed

2 fresh thyme sprigs

4 ripe tomatoes, chopped

100g (4oz) tomato purée

400ml (14fl oz) water

3 pinches of sugar (optional)

for the stuffing

20g (¾oz) unsalted butter

50g (2oz) onion, chopped

1 tsp fresh thyme leaves

1 fresh or dried bay leaf

100g (4oz) long grain rice

200ml (7fl oz) water

30g (1¼oz) carrot, very finely sliced

30g (1¼oz) each celery and courgette, finely sliced

30g (1¼oz) peas

2 tbsp whipping cream

75g (3oz) Gruyère, finely grated

Step one First make the tomato sauce. On a low heat, in a medium pan, heat the olive oil and add the onion, garlic and thyme, then soften for 2–3 minutes. Add the tomatoes and tomato purée, and cook on a medium heat for 7–8 minutes, until the tomatoes have cooked down. Add the water, season with 2 pinches of salt and a pinch of white pepper and cook for 5 minutes. Taste and adjust the seasoning, adding the sugar if necessary. Purée the sauce in a food-processor or blender (strain through a sieve as well if you want a very smooth sauce) and set aside.

Step two To prepare the tomatoes, slice about a third off the top of each tomato to make a hat; set this aside. With a spoon, scoop out the pulp and juices from the tomatoes into a bowl and set aside.

Step three To make the stuffing, melt the butter in a medium pan on a medium heat, add the onion, thyme and bay leaf, and soften for 3 minutes, without letting it colour. Stir in the rice and cook for 1 minute. Add the water, the sliced carrot, 150ml (¼ pint) of the reserved tomato pulp and juice, plus 2 pinches of salt and a pinch of white pepper. Bring to the boil, then reduce the heat to a gentle simmer and cook for 5 minutes, stirring from time to time.

Step four Preheat the oven to 180°C/350°F/gas 4. Add the celery, courgette and peas to the rice dish and cook for 15 minutes. Stir in the cream and grated cheese. Taste and adjust the seasoning, if necessary.

Step five Divide the rice stuffing among the tomatoes and top each of them with a tomato 'hat'. Place them in a baking dish, drizzle with the extra-virgin olive oil and bake for 20 minutes. To serve, reheat the tomato sauce and pour it into the baking dish around the stuffed tomatoes, or you can serve directly on individual plates. Garnish with snipped chives.

Baked Pancakes with Gruyère

A great, warming dish for all seasons. The stuffed pancakes can be prepared a day in advance, ready for baking, and they will be just as good.

Step one Heat the butter in a small pan until foaming and hazelnut brown. Allow to cool for 2 minutes. In a blender, liquidize the eggs, milk, flour, 4 pinches of salt and a pinch of black pepper for 1 minute, until smooth. Pour in the butter and liquidise for a further 30 seconds to incorporate it. Add the snipped chives and chopped parsley, transfer to a bowl, cover with clingfilm and set aside.

Step two Melt half the butter for the filling in a medium-sized frying pan on a high heat and add the spinach. Cook down at full heat, stirring all the time, for 2 minutes. Season with a pinch of each of salt and white pepper. With the back of the spoon, squeeze the water out of the spinach. Set the spinach aside. Melt the remaining butter in the same frying pan, add the mushrooms and cook for 2 minutes. Season then mix the mushrooms with the spinach, stir in the finely grated Gruyère and set aside.

Step three Preheat the oven to 200°C/400°F/gas 6. Heat a small frying pan or, better still, a pancake pan on a medium heat. Add a teaspoon of the oil and swirl it around. The oil must be hot enough to sear and cook the pancakes. Ladle just enough pancake batter into the hot pan to cover the surface when swirled. Cook for 15–20 seconds until browned underneath. Slide a spatula underneath and flip the pancake over. Cook for a further 15–20 seconds, then transfer to a baking sheet. Repeat, adding more oil as necessary, until all the batter has been used. You will need eight all together but you will probably end up with a few extra.

Step four Spoon the spinach and mushroom filling along each pancake and roll up tightly. Arrange all the rolled pancakes in the gratin dish. To make the cheese sauce, bring the whipping cream to a rolling boil and add 8 gratings of nutmeg, 2 pinches of salt and a pinch of white pepper. Pour the cream over the pancakes and grate the Gruyère cheese finely over the top. Bake for 20 minutes until the cheese has a golden-brown crust. Serve the bubbling dish from oven to table.

Serves 4

special equipment

a gratin dish roughly 25–30cm (10–12in) long

for the pancakes

50g (2oz) unsalted butter

2 eggs

200ml (7fl oz) whole milk

100g (4oz) plain flour

1 tbsp snipped fresh chives

1 tbsp chopped fresh flat-leaf parsley

1 tbsp groundnut oil or other unscented oil, for cooking the pancakes

for the filling

40g (1½oz) unsalted butter

300g (11oz) spinach leaves, washed, stalks removed, and dried

200g (7oz) button mushrooms, sliced 3mm (⅛in) thick

50g (2oz) Gruyère, finely grated

for the cream and cheese sauce

400ml (14fl oz) whipping cream

freshly grated nutmeg

50g (2oz) Gruyère

Semolina and Gruyère Quenelles

A quenelle is usually a fish or meat mousse enriched with cream and eggs, shaped into ovals with spoons and then poached. Here we use semolina and Gruyère cheese, and shape it more simply by rolling it.

Serves 4

special equipment

a 20cm (8in) oval gratin dish

for the quenelles

300ml (½ pint) milk

50g (2oz) unsalted butter, diced

100g (4oz) semolina

50g (2oz) plain flour

1 egg, plus 1 egg yolk

120g (4½ oz) Gruyère, finely grated

8 gratings of nutmeg

2 litres (3½ pints) water

for the tomato sauce

3 tbsp olive oil

1 onion, finely chopped

2 garlic cloves, crushed

2 fresh thyme sprigs

4 ripe tomatoes, de-seeded and chopped

100g (4oz) tomato purée

400ml (14fl oz) water

3 pinches of sugar (optional)

for the topping

50g (2oz) Gruyère, finely grated

Step one To make the quenelle mixture, bring the milk to simmering point in a medium-sized pan, then add the butter, semolina and flour all together. Stir with a wooden spoon for 2–3 minutes, until the mixture thickens; remove from the heat and stir in the egg, egg yolk and Gruyère. Season with the nutmeg, 3 pinches of salt and 2 pinches of pepper. With a palette knife, spread the mixture over a baking sheet. Leave to cool for 10 minutes, then cover with clingfilm and chill for at least 2 hours.

Step two To make the tomato sauce, heat the oil in a medium pan on a low heat and add the onion, garlic and thyme, then soften for 2–3 minutes. Add the tomatoes and tomato purée, and cook on a medium heat for 7–8 minutes. Add the water, season with 2 pinches of salt and a pinch of black pepper, and cook for 5 minutes. Taste and adjust the seasoning, adding the sugar if necessary. Purée the sauce in a food-processor or blender. Strain through a sieve if you want a very smooth sauce.

Step three Preheat the oven to 160°C/325°F/gas 3. Divide the quenelle mixture in half. With your hands, on a lightly floured work surface, roll each half into a big sausage shape, about 20 x 4cm (8 x 1½in). Cut each piece in half again to obtain four 10cm (4in) quenelles. In a large pan, bring the 2 litres (3½ pints) water to simmering point. Slide the quenelles carefully into the simmering water. They will sink to the bottom but will rise to the surface when cooked; this will take 8–10 minutes. With a fish slice, lift the cooked quenelles carefully onto kitchen paper to absorb excess water.

Step four Pour the tomato sauce into the gratin dish and arrange the quenelles in it. Sprinkle over the Gruyère for the topping and bake for 15 minutes, until the cheese has coloured lightly (put the dish under a hot grill for a few more minutes if necessary).

Tarte Tatin

All the elements of pleasure are here: the dark caramel, the sweet and acid taste of the apple, the crisp pastry. Serve with the very best crème fraîche (full fat, please) or a scoop of Vanilla Ice Cream (see page 175). The best way to eat it is an hour or so after cooking, when it is still warm.

Step one On a lightly floured surface, roll out the pastry to 2mm (¹⁄₁₆in) thick and prick it all over with a fork. Transfer to a baking sheet, cover with clingfilm and chill for 20–30 minutes to firm it up and prevent shrinkage during cooking. Cut out a 20cm (8in) circle, using a plate or cake tin as a template, prick with a fork and chill again.

Step two Preheat the oven to 190°C/375°F/gas 5. To make the caramel, put the water in a small, heavy-based pan and scatter the sugar over it in an even layer. Let the sugar absorb the water for a few minutes, then place the pan on a medium heat and leave, without stirring, until the sugar has dissolved and formed a syrup. Simmer until it turns to a golden brown caramel. Stir in the butter and immediately pour the caramel into the baking tin.

Step three Arrange 12 apple halves upright around the edge of the tin to complete a full circle. In the middle sit half an apple, flat-side up, then top with another half apple. Cut the remaining apple into slices and wedge them into the empty spaces. Brush the melted butter over the apples and sprinkle the caster sugar over the top. Bake for 35 minutes, until the apples are partly cooked.

Step four Remove from the oven, place the puff pastry circle on top of the hot apples and tuck the edge of the pastry inside the tin. Cook for a further 30 minutes, until the pastry is golden brown. Place the tarte Tatin next to an open window, if possible, and leave for 1–2 hours, until barely warm. Slide the blade of a sharp knife full circle inside the tin to release the tarte Tatin. Place a large dinner plate over the tart and, holding both tin and plate together, turn it upside down to release the tart onto the plate.

Serves 4

special equipment

an 18cm (7in) round baking tin, 4–5cm (1½–2in) deep

200g (7oz) shop-bought puff pastry, thawed if frozen

8 large Cox's apples, peeled, halved and cored with a melon baller

10g (⅓oz) unsalted butter, melted

1 tbsp caster sugar

for the caramel

50ml (2fl oz) water

100g (4oz) caster sugar

25g (1oz) unsalted butter

Summer Fruits Steeped in Red Wine, Monbazillac, Basil and Mint

A great summer favourite at Le Manoir. Many other fruits can be added, such as blackberries, blueberries and peaches. This dish can be prepared up to 1 day in advance.

Serves 4

250ml (8fl oz) Monbazillac or dessert wine

85ml (3fl oz) Cabernet Sauvignon

40g (1½ oz) caster sugar

5g (1 tsp) vanilla purée (see below)

8 fresh basil leaves

12 fresh mint leaves, roughly chopped

100ml (4fl oz) cold water

225g (8oz) raspberries

150g (5oz) strawberries, stems removed, quartered

100g (4oz) blackberries

¼ Charentais melon, scooped into 12 balls with a melon baller or diced

40g (1½ oz) wild strawberries (optional)

100ml (3½ fl oz) chilled pink champagne

4 fresh mint sprigs, to garnish

freshly ground black pepper

Step one In a small pan, mix the two wines, the sugar, vanilla purée and some black pepper. Wrap the basil and mint leaves in muslin and add them to the pan. Bring to the boil and boil for 1 minute. Then turn off the heat and add the cold water. Cool down to about 40°C/100°F. At this stage mix in all the fruits. Cover and chill for at least 6 hours, or up to 1 day.

Step two Remove the muslin bag of herbs. Place the soup and fruit into a large glass serving bowl or four individual glass bowls. Pour the pink champagne into the bowl or divide among each of the individual bowls and add the sprigs of mint.

To make Vanilla Purée, dissolve 60g (2oz) sugar in 60ml (2fl oz) water, bring to the boil and reduce to a syrup then set aside to cool. Chop up 6 whole vanilla pods and purée them in the cooled syrup using a liquidizer. Now you have your own vanilla syrup to use by the teaspoonful. If you must use vanilla essence instead, please use the best available with all natural ingredients.

Vanilla Crème Brûlée

The traditional recipe for crème brûlée, made with double cream, is rich and delicious. This recipe tastes just as good but is much lighter. This dish can be prepared 3 or 4 hours in advance.

Step one With a small sharp knife, split the vanilla pod lengthways. With the back of the blade, scrape off all the seeds inside the pod. Chop the pod finely. Bring the milk to the boil in a pan with the vanilla seeds and chopped pod, then cook at a gentle simmer for a further 5 minutes. Turn off the heat and set aside.

Step two In a mixing bowl, whisk together the egg yolks and caster sugar until a pale straw colour. Pour the hot milk onto the egg yolk mixture. Mix well, then strain the milk and egg yolk mixture through a fine sieve into a clean pan, pressing on the vanilla pods and seeds to extract as much flavour as possible. Spoon off any foam from the surface and set aside.

Step three Preheat the oven to 140°C/275°F/gas 1. Pour equal quantities of the mixture into the ramekins or egg dishes. Line a deep roasting tin or dish just large enough to hold the ramekins with kitchen paper. Place the filled ramekins into this, on top of the paper. (Placing kitchen paper under the ramekins during cooking will serve as a form of insulation against the strong heat from the oven and prevent them from overcooking.) Add enough boiling water to the tin or dish to reach three-quarters of the height of the ramekins. Transfer the tin to the oven and bake for about 30 minutes until the mixture has just set. When the mixture has set, remove each ramekin from the water and leave to cool down at room temperature. When cold, chill for at least 1 hour.

Step four Preheat the grill to very hot. Sprinkle the demerara sugar over the top of each cream, and caramelise under the hot grill for 2–3 minutes according to its strength. Leave to cool and set into a delightful layer of crisp caramel. When set, place the ramekins on serving plates and serve.

Serves 4

special equipment

4 ramekins 10cm (4in) in diameter, or 2 white china egg dishes

1 vanilla pod

300ml (½ pint) milk

4 egg yolks

40g (1½ oz) caster sugar

40g (1½ oz) demerara sugar

163

Apple Tart 'Maman Blanc'

'Maman Blanc' loves simplicity, and this tart is easy to prepare as the pastry case does not need to be pre-baked.

Serves 6

special equipment

tart tin 18cm (7in) in diameter, 2cm (¾in) deep, with removable base

for the pastry

250g (90z) plain flour

120g (4½ oz) butter, diced, at room temperature

1 egg

sea salt

for the filling

1 tbsp melted butter

½ tbsp lemon juice

1 tbsp caster sugar

½ tbsp Calvados (optional) mixed together

3 apples (such as Cox, Worcester, Russet or Braeburn), peeled, cored and cut into 10 segments

icing sugar, for dusting

Step one In a large bowl and using your fingertips, rub together the flour, butter and a pinch of salt until it reaches a sandy texture. Make a well in the centre and add the egg. Work the egg into the mixture, then press together to form a ball. Line a work surface with clingfilm and knead the dough with the palms of your hands for 30 seconds, until you have a homogeneous consistency. Do not overwork the dough or the pastry will lose some of its flakiness. Take off about 25g (1oz) of dough, wrap it in clingfilm and store for later. Wrap the remaining dough in clingfilm and flatten it slightly to 2cm (¾in) thickness, then leave to rest in the fridge for 30 minutes.

Step two Place a baking sheet in the oven and preheat the oven to 220°C/425°F/gas 7. Line a work surface with clingfilm. Take the pastry dough from the fridge, unwrap it and place it on a piece of clingfilm about 30 x 30cm (12 x 12in). Cover it with another layer of clingfilm and roll the dough out to 3mm (⅛in) thick. Line the tart tin with the dough. Then unwrap the piece of spare dough and press this into the corner between the base and side of the tin to ensure the pastry is neatly compressed and moulded to the shape of the tin. Trim the edges of the tart. Raise the height of the dough 3mm (⅛ in) above the tart tin by pressing and pinching the pastry gently all round the edge of the tin using your index finger and thumb. Prick the bottom of the tart, then rest in the fridge for 20 minutes.

Step three Mix together all the ingredients for the filling except the apples and icing sugar. Lay the apple segments, closely together, in the base of the pastry case. Brush with the melted butter, sugar and lemon juice mixture, and dust liberally with icing sugar. Slide the tart into the oven, onto the preheated baking sheet, and cook for 10 minutes. Turn the oven down to 200°C/400°F/gas 6 and cook for a further 20 minutes, until the pastry becomes a light golden colour and the apples have caramelised. Remove the tart from the oven and allow to cool for a minimum of 1 hour before serving.

Black Cherry Tart

The sweet pastry must be made at least 2 hours in advance and can also be prepared the day before. This type of pastry is suitable for freezing.

Step one First make the sweet pastry. In a bowl, beat the butter until a white 'cream' has formed. Beat in the icing sugar and egg yolks. Sift in the plain flour and, with your fingertips, rub in until you obtain a sandy texture. Press together. Place the mixture on a work surface and with the palm of your hand knead to a smooth dough. Wrap the dough in clingfilm and allow to rest in the fridge for at least 2 hours.

Step two Preheat the oven to 180°C/350°F/gas 4. With a pastry brush, grease the inside of the tart tin with the softened unsalted butter. Set aside. On a lightly floured surface, roll the sweet pastry out into a 25cm (10in) circle. Place the circle onto the tart tin and press it down into the tin using your thumb. Use the blade of a knife to trim any excess at the top on the rim.

Step three Mix together the sugar and flour, and sprinkle the mixture over the bottom of the pastry-lined tin (this mixture will absorb the juice produced by the cherries during cooking). Place the pitted cherries on the base of the tart tin, and bake for about 30–40 minutes. Remove from the oven and leave to cool on a wire rack. When cool, remove the sides of the tin and place the tart on a serving dish. Cut into wedges at the table.

Serves 4

special equipment

a tart tin with removable base, 18cm (7in) in diameter, 2.5cm (1in) in height

20g (¾oz) unsalted butter, softened

2 tbsp caster sugar

1 tbsp plain flour

350g (12oz) black cherries, pitted

for the sweet pastry

60g (2¼oz) unsalted butter

30g (1¼oz) icing sugar

2 egg yolks

120g (4½oz) plain flour

Grand Marnier Soufflé

One of the great classic soufflés. Try it first on your long-suffering family or trusted friends.

Serves 4

special equipment

1 large soufflé dish
15cm (6in) wide x 6cm
(2¼ in) deep

for the soufflé dish

1 tsp butter, at room
temperature

20g (¾oz) caster
sugar

for the soufflé

100ml (4fl oz) warm
pastry cream (see
below)

30ml (1¼ fl oz) Grand
Marnier

finely grated zest of
¼ orange

5 egg whites

60g (2¼ oz) caster
sugar

icing sugar, for dusting

Step one Preheat the oven to 170°C/340°F/gas 3–4 with a baking sheet on the middle shelf. Using a pastry brush, butter the inside of the soufflé dish. Sprinkle the sugar inside and rotate it until completely coated. Shake out the excess.

Step two In a bowl mix together the pastry cream, Grand Marnier and orange zest, and keep warm by resting the bowl over a pan of steaming water. In a separate bowl, whisk the egg whites to soft peaks, then gradually add the sugar and whisk until firm but not too stiff. Whisk a quarter of the egg whites into the warm pastry cream until smooth. Using a spatula, briskly fold in the remaining egg whites by cutting and lifting with large circular movements.

Step three Fill the soufflé dish to the top. Smooth off the surface with a palette knife. Sprinkle the top with icing sugar, leave to melt for 1 minute and repeat. Run your thumb round the edge to neaten. Transfer to the baking sheet in the oven and bake for 20 minutes.

To make 600ml (1 pint) pastry cream, in a medium-sized pan, bring 500ml (¾ pint) milk to a simmer. Meanwhile, in a large mixing bowl, whisk 6 egg yolks, 50g (2oz) caster sugar and 1 tsp vanilla purée; then, whisk in 80g (3oz) flour. Gradually add the hot milk and continue to whisk. Pour the mixture into the saucepan and, on a medium heat, bring to the boil, whisking constantly for about 1 minute until you obtain a smooth consistency. Pour immediately into a bowl and sprinkle with caster sugar to prevent a crust forming. Once cool, cover with cling film and refrigerate.

Cherry Clafoutis

Clafoutis is a great family dish. Everyone should know how to make this dessert. It is so easy to prepare and your children, husband, wife and friends will love you two thousand times more for it. Put the clafoutis in the oven just before you sit down to eat your meal, then it will be at the right temperature when you serve it; just warm is best.

Step one Mix the cherries with 2 tablespoons of the caster sugar and the kirsch, if using, and leave for 2 hours to maximise their flavour.

Step two Brush the inside of the baking dish with the melted butter. Sprinkle in the remaining 3 tablespoons of caster sugar and shake the dish so it coats the inside evenly. This will give the clafoutis a lovely crust during cooking. Preheat the oven to 180°C/350°F/gas 4.

Step three To make the batter, put the flour and salt in a mixing bowl and make a well in the centre. Add the eggs, egg yolk, sugar, lemon zest and the vanilla, if using. With a whisk, slowly incorporate the egg mixture into the flour until smooth. Whisk in the milk and cream. In a small pan, heat the butter until it turns a pale hazelnut colour, then whisk it into the batter while still hot.

Step four Mix the cherries and their juices into the batter and then pour into the baking dish. Bake for 30–35 minutes, until the blade of a knife inserted into the mixture comes out completely clean. Sprinkle a little caster sugar over and serve warm.

Serves 4

special equipment

a round or oval cast-iron or china baking dish, 20cm (8in) in diameter and 5cm (2in) deep

500g (1lb 2oz) fresh cherries, stoned

5 tbsp caster sugar, plus extra to sprinkle

2 tbsp kirsch (optional)

10g (⅓oz) unsalted butter, melted

for the batter

100g (4oz) plain white flour

a pinch of salt

3 eggs plus 1 egg yolk

6 tbsp caster sugar

finely grated zest of 1 lemon

6 drops of natural vanilla extract (optional)

150ml (¼ pint) milk

150ml (¼ pint) whipping cream

75g (3oz) unsalted butter

Floating Islands 'Maman Blanc'

A dessert from my childhood – a big treat for children and grown-ups.

Serves 4–6

1.25 litres (2¼ pints) full-fat milk

2 vanilla pods, split lengthways

for the meringue

8 egg whites

275g (10oz) caster sugar

for the vanilla custard

8 egg yolks

75g (3oz) caster sugar

milk from poaching the meringue

for the caramel

50ml (2fl oz) water

150g (5oz) caster sugar

Step one Pour the milk into a large, shallow pan, about 30cm (12in) in diameter and 7.5cm (3in) deep, and bring to simmering point. Scrape the vanilla seeds into the milk with the point of a sharp knife and whisk to disperse them; add the split vanilla pods, too. Bring to the boil and reduce the heat to a slow simmer, then simmer for 5 minutes to infuse the milk.

Step two To make the meringue, whisk the egg whites and sugar with an electric beater on full power for at least 10 minutes, until the mixture forms shiny, firm peaks.

Step three With a large spoon, carefully scoop out four or six large chunks of whisked egg white. Poach in the gently simmering milk for 5 minutes on each side, taking great care not to damage the delicate meringue when turning it over. Carefully lift the poached meringue onto a baking sheet and set aside. Strain the milk into a pan.

Step four To make the custard, in a large bowl whisk the egg yolks with the caster sugar, then gradually whisk in the hot milk. Pour the mixture back into the pan. Cook over a medium heat for 4–5 minutes, until the custard begins to thicken. Stir constantly and lift the spoon every 10–15 seconds to check if the sauce is thickening (when it is ready it will coat the back of the spoon). Strain into a large bowl and continue stirring for 2 minutes to stop any further cooking, otherwise the custard could scramble. Leave to cool, then chill. Pour the custard into a large serving bowl and, using a fish slice, carefully place the poached meringues on top .

Step five To make the caramel, put the water in a small, heavy-based pan and scatter the sugar over it in an even layer. Let the sugar absorb the water for a few minutes, then place the pan on a medium heat and leave, without stirring, until the sugar has dissolved and formed a syrup. Simmer until it turns to a golden brown caramel. Immediately place the bottom of the pan in cold water to stop the caramel cooking any further. Pour a fine coating of caramel over the poached meringues. Wait a few seconds until the caramel sets before serving.

Vanilla Ice Cream

For this recipe you will need an ice-cream machine. It will be a very good investment as you will be able to prepare so many easy ice creams, sorbets and desserts in very little time. These are very much better than many bought versions, most of which are full of emulsifiers, additives, colourings, flavourings and far too much sugar. Maturing the cream in the fridge for 24 hours before freezing will improve both its taste and texture.

Step one In a large mixing bowl, cream together the egg yolks, sugar and dried milk until a pale straw colour. Pour the milk into a heavy-based pan. Halve the vanilla pod lengthways and scrape the seeds out into the milk. Chop the pod very finely, and add to the milk as well. Bring to the boil, then simmer for about 5 minutes.

Step two Bring the milk back to the boil and pour it onto the egg, sugar and dried milk mixture, whisking continuously. Return the mixture to the pan on a medium heat. Stir the custard until it thickens and coats the back of your spoon. Strain immediately through a sieve into a bowl, pressing down on the vanilla to get as much flavour as possible, then stir for a few minutes. Put the bowl into another bowl filled with ice, and cool, before churning in the ice-cream machine.

Serves 6–8

special equipment

an ice-cream machine

8 egg yolks

120g (4½oz) caster sugar

4 tsp dried milk

500ml (17fl oz) milk

1 vanilla pod

Peaches Poached in White Wine and Citrus Fruits

The perfect dessert when peaches are in season. White peaches have the very best flavour and for that there is a small extra price to pay.

Serves 4

8 ripe but firm peaches, white if possible

1 orange

½ lemon

175g (6oz) caster sugar

500ml (17fl oz) water

500ml (17fl oz) dry white wine

1 vanilla pod, split lengthways and seeds scraped out

8 fresh sprigs spearmint

Step one Remove the stalks from the peaches. Cut the orange and lemon into fine slices about 3mm (⅛in) thick, leaving the rind on.

Step two Place the peaches in a large pan in a single layer. Add the caster sugar, water, white wine, vanilla pod and seeds. Top with the orange and lemon slices. Cut out a round of greaseproof paper the same size as the pan and cut a hole in the centre to allow excess steam to escape. Place it directly on top of the peaches.

Step three On a high heat, bring to the boil. Immediately reduce the heat to a gentle simmer and cook for about 20 minutes (the flesh of peaches is very delicate; if subjected to high heat, their texture will be ruined, so cook them very gently). There is an easy way to see if the peaches are cooked or not: you will notice some tiny bubbles escaping from the point where you removed the stalk; when these bubbles stop coming out, the peach is ready. Turn off the heat and leave the peaches to cool in the liquid.

Step four Chop 4 of the spearmint sprigs and mix them into the cooled syrup. Chill for at least 6 hours and up to 24, to allow the exchange of flavours among the citrus, spearmint and peaches.

Step five With a slotted spoon, transfer the peaches to a plate and carefully peel off the skin. Place the peaches, orange and lemon slices and vanilla pod in a glass serving bowl and pour the white wine and citrus syrup over (if you have too much syrup, freeze it and scrape beautiful frozen flakes of it into glasses to serve as a pre-dessert at a future meal). Arrange the remaining 4 spearmint sprigs on top.

Medley of Summer Fruits in Raspberry and Strawberry Sauce

This dessert should be prepared a maximum of 5 hours in advance of your meal.

Step one First prepare the red fruit sauce. Trim, wash and drain the fruit, then place it in a blender. Add most of the sugar and lemon juice, and purée. Force the pulp through a fine sieve into a large mixing bowl. Taste, add more sugar and lemon juice if necessary, then set aside.

Step two Wash and drain the fruit. Wash and drain the mint leaves, and remove their stems. Cut each peach into eight segments and set aside. Halve the melon, remove the seeds and divide each half into six. Remove the peel, and cut each piece into two lengthways. Cut large strawberries into halves and quarters, leaving smaller ones whole.

Step three Mix all the fruit together and place in the sauce. Chop the mint leaves very finely and mix with the fruit. Cover with clingfilm and chill for at least 1 hour. After chilling, taste the fruit mixture and add a little sugar if necessary. To serve, place the fruit and sauce into a glass bowl, and serve while very cold. You can add a festive note by pouring a little Champagne on to each fruit medley in front of your guests. This will produce a beautiful foam and add to the freshness of the dish.

Serves 4

2 ripe peaches

1 small melon (Charentais)

100g (4oz) each of fresh raspberries, strawberries, blackcurrants and blackberries

8 fresh mint leaves

caster sugar, to taste

for the red fruit sauce

200g (7oz) fresh raspberries

200g (7oz) fresh strawberries

100g (4oz) caster sugar

juice of ½ lemon

100ml (3½ fl oz) Champagne (optional)

Pain Perdu with Warm Raspberries and Strawberries

Pain perdu means 'lost bread' (in England it is often known as French toast), and this recipe was devised as a means of using up leftover bread. The red fruits can be replaced by apples or peaches, in which case you will need to increase the cooking time by up to 5 minutes for apples or 3 minutes for peaches.

Serves 4

2 large eggs

50g (2oz) caster sugar

100ml (3½ fl oz) full-fat milk

2 tsp rum or cognac (optional)

a few drops of best-quality vanilla extract (optional)

4 slices of bread, cut 2cm (¾ in) thick, crusts removed, cut in half

40g (1½ oz) unsalted butter

shredded fresh mint, to decorate

for the warm raspberries and strawberries

2 tbsp water

50g (2oz) caster sugar

25g (1oz) chilled unsalted butter, diced

100g (4oz) strawberries, cut in half (or quartered if large)

100g (4oz) raspberries

2 tsp kirsch or cognac

Step one In a large bowl, beat the eggs with the sugar until the sugar has dissolved. Gradually mix in the milk and the rum or cognac and vanilla extract, if using. Place the slices of bread in a large dish and pour over the egg mixture. Allow the bread to soak for 4–5 minutes, then turn the slices over and soak for a further 4–5 minutes to ensure that all the liquid is absorbed. Carefully lift the bread from the dish with a fish slice and place on a baking sheet. Meanwhile, preheat the oven to 150°C/300°F/gas 2.

Step two On a medium heat, in a large frying pan, melt half the 40g (1½oz) butter. When it is foaming, add two bread slices and fry for 2 minutes on each side. Remove from the pan and set aside. Clean the pan, return it to the heat, melt the remaining butter and cook the remaining bread. Place on a baking sheet and bake for 5 minutes.

Step three To prepare the fruit, put the water in a medium frying pan and scatter the sugar over it in an even layer. Let the sugar absorb the water for a few minutes, then place the pan on a medium heat and leave, without stirring, until the sugar has dissolved and formed a syrup. Simmer until the syrup turns into a very pale blond caramel.

Step four Stir the diced butter into the caramel, add the strawberries and raspberries, then the kirsch or cognac, and cook for 30 seconds to soften the fruit and create delicious juices. To serve, remove the hot slices of bread from the oven and place on four plates. Spoon the warm strawberries and raspberries over the bread and spoon the red fruit syrup around, then decorate with a little shredded mint.

Lemon Tart

Making this tart is quite a lengthy process but relatively simple – and worth it.

Step one To make the pastry, with a spatula or wooden spoon, mix the soft butter and icing sugar to a cream; then beat in two of the egg yolks. Add the flour and, with your fingertips, rub the mixture together to achieve a crumbly texture. Add the water and press the mixture together to form a ball. With the palms of your hands, knead the pastry on a lightly floured work surface until it is blended (maximum 30 seconds). Flatten the pastry slightly with the palm of your hand, wrap in clingfilm and chill for 30 minutes.

Step two To make the lemon cream, in a large bowl, mix together the eggs, sugar, lemon juice and zest, and whisk for a few seconds. Add the cream whisk it in, then place in the fridge.

Step three Roll out the pastry on a lightly floured work surface, into a circle 3mm (⅛ in) thick. Roll the pastry over the rolling pin and unroll it over the loose-bottomed tart tin. With one hand, lift the pastry and with the other gently tuck it into the bottom edge of the tin so that it fits tightly. Be careful not to stretch it. Cut off excess pastry by rolling the pin over the top edge of the tin. Take a small ball of pastry and gently press it all around the base of the tart to ensure a snug fit. Prick the base of the pastry all over with a fork and chill for 30 minutes. Meanwhile, preheat the oven to 160°C/ 325°F/gas 3.

Step four Line the pastry case with foil and baking beans, and bake blind for 10 minutes, then remove from the oven and lift out both foil and beans. Return the tart tin to the oven and bake for a further 20 minutes. Brush the inside of the pastry with the remaining egg yolk and return to the oven for 1 minute. Turn the oven down to 140°C/ 275°F/gas 1.

Step five Pour the lemon mixture into a pan and warm gently. Pour the warm mixture into the pastry case and bake for 25 minutes, until barely set. Remove the tart from the oven and leave to cool for at least 1 hour, then dredge with icing sugar and remove from the tin onto a plate.

Serves 4–6

special equipment
a 24cm (9½ in) loose-bottomed tart tin

for the sweet pastry
120g (4½ oz) unsalted butter, at room temperature, diced

75g (3oz) icing sugar, sifted, plus extra for dusting

3 egg yolks

250g (9oz) plain flour

2 tbsp water

for the lemon cream
5 eggs

150g (5oz) caster sugar

85ml (3fl oz) lemon juice

2 tbsp finely grated lemon zest

150ml (¼ pint) double cream

Millefeuilles of Shortbread and Raspberries

The shortbread pastry must be made at least 2 hours in advance, but can also be prepared the day before.

Serves 4

special equipment

a fluted pastry cutter 9cm (3½ in) in diameter

300g (11oz) ripe fresh raspberries

20g (¾ oz) icing sugar

for the shortbread pastry

50g (2oz) icing sugar, sifted

1 egg yolk

100g (4oz) unsalted butter, creamed

135g (4¾ oz) plain flour, sifted

a pinch of salt

for the raspberry sauce

250g (9oz) ripe fresh raspberries

40g (1½ oz) caster sugar

juice of ¼ lemon

Step one To make the shortbread pastry, in a bowl mix together the icing sugar, egg yolk, creamed butter and a pinch of salt. Add the flour and rub together using your fingertips until sandy in texture. Press together to a fairly soft dough.

Step two Lightly flour a work surface and place the dough on it. Knead with the palm of your hand until it is well blended. Wrap in clingfilm and chill for at least 2 hours to allow the dough to firm up.

Step three To make the raspberry sauce, place the fruit, sugar and lemon juice in a bowl and slightly mash with a fork. Marinate for about an hour. When marinated, liquidise in a blender and then rub through a sieve into a bowl, pressing out as much purée as possible with a ladle. Set aside in the fridge.

Step four Preheat the oven to 160°C/325°F/gas 3. On a lightly floured surface, roll the shortbread pastry out into a rectangle 37 x 28cm (14¾ x 11¼in). With a fluted pastry cutter, cut out 12 discs. Using a palette knife, carefully slide the discs onto a baking sheet, placing them slightly apart from each other to allow for spread. Bake for 10–15 minutes or until a light blond colour. Remove from the oven and leave to cool on a wire rack.

Step five Pour 2 tablespoons of the raspberry sauce into a very large bowl, then add the fresh raspberries. Shake to coat the raspberries. Set aside. When ready to serve, divide the marinated raspberries into two portions. Take four of the pastry discs and place in the centre of four plates. Divide half the raspberries evenly among the four discs. Place another pastry disc on top of the layer of raspberries. Divide the remaining raspberries evenly among the discs. Lightly dust the four remaining shortbread discs with icing sugar and place them on top of the last layer of raspberries. Pour the remaining raspberry sauce around the dessert and serve.

Chocolate Mousse

Do use the very best chocolate, with 70 per cent cocoa solids, and also the very best unsweetened cocoa powder for this simple but delicious chocolate mousse recipe.

Serves 4

165g (5½ oz) dark chocolate, at least 70% cocoa solids, finely chopped

25g (1oz) unsweetened cocoa powder

10 egg whites, plus 1 egg yolk

25g (1oz) caster sugar

fresh mint sprigs, to garnish

Step one Place the chocolate and cocoa powder in a large bowl set over a pan of hot water and leave to melt over a low heat; do not boil the water or the chocolate will become grainy. Stir until smooth, then remove from the heat. Keep warm over the pan of water.

Step two With an electric beater, whisk the egg whites and sugar for 2–3 minutes, until they form soft peaks. Stir the egg yolk into the chocolate and cocoa mixture, and immediately whisk in a quarter of the egg whites to lighten the mixture. Fold in the remaining egg whites with a large spatula, ensuring that you do not over mix or the mousse will be heavy.

Step three Pour into a glass bowl or individual glasses and leave to set in the fridge for 2 hours or until required. Garnish with a sprig of fresh mint before serving.

Crème Caramel

There are two points to watch when making crème caramel: first, the caramel must be allowed to turn a deep brown, almost to the point of burning – too pale and it will taste sweet with no caramel flavour; too dark and it will be bitter. Second, the custard mixture should be cooked until it is only just set, otherwise you will lose that magical melting-snow effect in the mouth.

Serves 4

special equipment

4 ramekins, about 7.5cm (3in) in diameter and 5cm (2in) deep

for the caramel

2 tbsp water

120g (4½oz) caster sugar

for the custard mixture

500ml (17fl oz) full-fat milk

½ vanilla pod, split lengthways and seeds removed, or ½ tsp natural vanilla extract

2 eggs, plus 3 egg yolks

100g (4oz) caster sugar

Step one Put the water in a small, heavy-based pan and scatter the sugar over it in an even layer. Let the sugar absorb the water for a few minutes, then place the pan on a medium heat and leave, without stirring, until the sugar has dissolved and formed a syrup. Simmer until the syrup turns into a rich brown caramel. Wrap a cloth around your hand and immediately remove the pan from the heat. Pour the caramel into the ramekins; tilt each ramekin slightly so the caramel coats the base evenly. Transfer the ramekins to a baking tin and set aside.

Step two Preheat the oven to 160°C/325°F/gas 3. To make the custard mixture, put the milk in a pan with the vanilla pod and seeds (or vanilla extract) and bring just to simmering point for 3–4 minutes to allow the milk to become infused with the vanilla. Meanwhile, in a large bowl, lightly whisk the eggs and egg yolks with the sugar. Slowly pour in the hot milk, whisking all the time.

Step three Strain the mixture through a fine sieve into the caramel-lined ramekins. Place the baking tin containing the ramekins in the oven and carefully pour enough boiling water into the tin to come two-thirds of the way up the side of the ramekins. Bake for 55–60 minutes, until the crème caramels are just set (press gently with your finger to check). Any dip in the centre means they are undercooked.

Step four Remove from the oven and leave to cool, then chill for 2 hours (or overnight, if more convenient). To release each crème caramel from the dish, take a thin, sharp knife and slide it around the inside edge of the ramekin, then turn it out onto a serving plate.

Strawberry Sorbet

Only use the sweetest seasonal strawberries for this recipe. I always look forward to the first Gaurigette strawberries in France, while we wait for the British strawberries to ripen enough to be picked. This recipe can be adapted to any soft berries, but always taste your fruit and adjust the sugar according to the sweetness.

Step one Wash the fruit briefly under cold running water while the stems are still in place. Drain and dry on kitchen paper. Pull or cut off the stems, then slice the fruit. Place in a bowl and sprinkle with the caster sugar and lemon juice. Mix and leave to marinate for 30 minutes at room temperature.

Step two Liquidise the strawberry mixture and pass it through a fine sieve. Place in the ice-cream machine and churn until frozen. Keep in the freezer until ready to serve.

Serves 3–4

special equipment
an ice-cream machine

450g (1lb) ripe fresh strawberries

80g (3¼ oz) caster sugar

a dash of lemon juice

Poached Pears with Cassis Coulis

The pears have to be poached at least 2 hours in advance to allow them to cool down in their juices; they can be poached the day before and kept in the fridge until served. The blackcurrant (cassis) coulis can be prepared up to a day in advance and kept in the fridge until served.

Serves 4

special equipment

a Parisian scoop

an 18cm (7in) stainless steel pan

an 18cm (7in) disc of greaseproof paper

4 ripe pears, about 175g (6oz) each (use Guyot or Williams)

1 litre (1¾ pints) water

200g (7oz) caster sugar

½ vanilla pod

juice of ½ lemon

for the blackcurrant coulis

1 litre (1¾ pints) water

250g (9oz) fresh blackcurrants (weighed after picking from stalks)

50g (2oz) caster sugar

Step one With a potato peeler, peel the pears very carefully, leaving the stalk on and not marking the fruit too deeply. Set aside. In the stainless steel pan, bring the water, caster sugar and vanilla pod to the boil. Place the peeled pears and lemon juice into the pan and cover with a disc of greaseproof paper. Bring back to the boil and simmer for 4–6 minutes. Remove the pan from the heat and leave the pears to cool in the cooking juices for about 2 hours or until they are at room temperature. Set aside in the fridge if you are not serving the pears immediately.

Step two To prepare the blackcurrant coulis, bring the water to the boil in a large pan. Put 200g (7oz) of the blackcurrants into the boiling water for about 20 seconds, then drain through a sieve. Place the partly cooked blackcurrants into a liquidiser or food-processor and liquidise. Pass through a sieve into a bowl, pressing as much as you can out of the purée. Stir in the sugar and if the purée is too thick, loosen with a little water.

Step three Drain the pears from their cooking juices. If you like, using a Parisian scoop, you can very carefully remove the core from each pear. Trim the wide bottom of each pear slightly to allow them to stand up. Place each one in the centre of a plate. In a small container, place 2 tablespoons of the blackcurrant coulis and the remaining fresh blackcurrants. Mix gently to coat the blackcurrants. Pour the remaining blackcurrant coulis equally around each pear, then sprinkle around the coated fresh blackcurrants, and serve.

Riz au Lait

Riz au lait is what the British call rice pudding. It is a timeless classic dish from French home cooking, both for children and adults. Every mother has her own recipe, which she hands down through her family, and of course hers is always the best. I had a serious 'argument' with my chef pâtissier, M. Benoit, whose mother's recipe was entirely different from mine, about whose recipe was best, and I won – sorry, my mother won! You can bake the rice pudding 1–2 hours in advance and serve it warm rather than hot. It can be served with poached pears or peaches in vanilla.

Step one Preheat the oven to 150°C/300°F/gas 2. On a medium heat, in a medium pan, bring the milk, sugar, vanilla pod and seeds (or vanilla extract) to the boil. Add the rice and return to a medium boil. On a medium–high heat, cook for 30 minutes, stirring every 5 minutes. Towards the end of the cooking, as the milk becomes more condensed and the consistency thickens, stir every 2 minutes or so to prevent the rice sticking to the bottom of the pan.

Step two Pour the rice into the baking dish and bake for 30 minutes.

Step three Preheat the grill. Remove the pudding from the oven and sprinkle caster or icing sugar over the top so it is completely covered. Caramelise under the hot grill for 1 minute.

Serves 4

special equipment

a shallow baking dish about 24cm (9¼ in) in diameter

850ml (28fl oz) full-fat milk

50g (2oz) caster sugar

1 vanilla pod, split lengthways and seeds scraped out, or a few drops of natural vanilla extract

75g (3oz) short grain (pudding) rice, washed in cold water and drained

caster sugar or icing sugar, for sprinkling

Stuffed Poached Figs with Port Ice Cream

The figs must be marinated for 24 hours in advance for best results.

Serves 6

special equipment

an ice-cream machine

stainless steel pan 28–30cm (11¼–12in) in diameter, plus a circle of greaseproof paper of the same diameter

500ml (17fl oz) dark cooking port

500ml (17fl oz) Sauternes or other sweet white wine

50g (2oz) whole blackcurrants, crushed

24 figs (purple are the best), untrimmed

for the port ice cream

4 egg yolks

50g (2oz) caster sugar

50ml (2fl oz) double cream

2 tsp dried milk

250ml (8fl oz) milk

250ml (8fl oz) port and fig purée (see step three)

Step one In the stainless steel pan bring the port, Sauternes and blackcurrants to the boil. Add the figs, top with the circle of greaseproof paper, and bring back to the boil. Reduce the heat and simmer for 2–5 minutes, then allow to cool to room temperature. Allow to marinate for 24 hours.

Step two Drain the figs from their marinating juices, and set the liquid aside. Trim off the stalks and, placing the figs sideways on your work surface, chop off the top third of each, creating a little hat. Do this to 18 figs only. Reserve the remaining six figs for the port and fig purée. Placing the hats sideways, and using the flat part of the blade of a knife, push out the fig flesh, keeping the outside skin intact. This is a delicate process. Reserve the trimmings, flesh and seeds. Place the bases, still holding their flesh, and the 'empty' hats on a small tray, and chill until required.

Step three To prepare the port and fig purée, sieve the marinating liquid into a container, pressing on the blackcurrants with a ladle to obtain as much juice as possible (you should have approximately 1 litre/1¾ pints of juice). Place the liquid, the fig trimmings and the six remaining figs into a pan, bring to the boil and reduce down slowly to 500ml (17fl oz). Liquidise, then set aside.

Step four To prepare the port ice cream, follow the Vanilla Ice Cream recipe on page 175, adding the hot unflavoured milk to the egg yolk mixture. When the sauce has cooled, whisk in 250ml (8fl oz) of the port and fig purée. Churn in the ice-cream machine for about 10–15 minutes. Reserve in the freezer.

Step five To serve, divide the remaining port and fig purée among six serving plates. Using a teaspoon, cover each fig base with port ice-cream. Top each fig with a hat, allowing the ice cream to be seen, and arrange three of these per prepared plate.

Banana Soufflé

This dish is suitable for those on a gluten-free diet or for diabetics if sugar is used neither to coat the inside of the mould, nor in the banana soufflé mix. The butter can be replaced by unsalted margarine.

Step one Preheat the oven to 170°C/325–350°F/gas 3–4. To prepare the ramekins, butter the inside of each ramekin with a pastry brush, then sprinkle in the caster sugar. Swirl the sugar around until each ramekin is coated. Set aside.

Step two Chop the bananas, then liquidise them with half the lemon juice to a very fine purée. Set aside. Place the egg whites and a few drops of the remaining lemon juice into an electric mixer and whisk to soft peaks. Gradually add the caster sugar (if using) and the remaining lemon juice and whisk until firmer peaks are reached.

Step three Whisk one-quarter of the whipped egg whites into the banana mixture, then fold in the remainder carefully until well incorporated. Fill the prepared ramekins with the soufflé mixture and smooth over the top with a palette knife. Run your thumb around the edge of the soufflé to push the mixture away from the sides. Place the ramekins on a baking sheet and bake for 8–10 minutes. Serve immediately.

Serves 4

special equipment

4 ramekins, 9cm (3½in) in diameter, 4.5cm (1¾in) deep

275g (10oz) very ripe banana flesh (about 3 bananas)

juice of ½ lemon

4 egg whites

30g (1¼oz) caster sugar (optional)

for the ramekins

30g (1¼oz) unsalted butter or margarine, softened

20g (¾oz) caster sugar

Hot Orange Buns

The bun mixture can be made up to a half a day in advance and kept covered in the fridge until needed.

Makes 6–8 buns

special equipment

6 large 'bun' moulds, muffin moulds or cake tins, which contain about 20ml (¾ fl oz) each

40g (1½ oz) unsalted butter, softened

finely grated zest of 1 orange

finely grated zest of ½ lemon

50g (2oz) caster sugar

1 egg

1 tbsp milk

70g (2¾ oz) self-raising flour

a pinch of salt

for the bun moulds

50g (2oz) unsalted butter, softened

2 tbsp plain flour

Step one In a medium bowl, cream the butter until soft. Whisk in the orange and lemon zests and the caster sugar. Add the egg, milk and a pinch of salt, and whisk again. Fold in the self-raising flour. Rest in the fridge for at least an hour.

Step two Pre-heat the oven to 180°C/350°F/gas 4. With a pastry brush, coat the inside of each mould or tin generously with the soft butter and dust with the plain flour. Shake off the excess flour and place the moulds in the fridge for 15 minutes to allow the butter to set.

Step three With a tablespoon, fill the prepared moulds up to the top with the bun mixture and bake for about 12 minutes until a light blond colour. The buns should have a spongy texture, and a crust should have built up underneath. Remove the cooked buns from the moulds or tin, and allow to cool a little on a wire rack. Serve while still warm.

Galette des Rois

This dessert is served just once a year, on 6 January (Epiphany). It makes a marvellous party dessert, as traditionally two little figurines can be hidden in the almond cream. The ones who find them become king and queen for the day and, of course, have all of their wishes granted. Two crowns would be perfectly fitting for the winners.

Step one On a lightly floured work surface, roll out the puff pastry into a 50 x 30cm (20 x 12in) rectangle, 2mm ($\frac{1}{16}$ in) thick. Transfer to a baking sheet, cover with clingfilm and place in the fridge for 30 minutes to firm up the pastry and prevent shrinkage while cooking. Then cut out two 20cm (8in) circles, using a plate or cake tin as a template, and chill again for at least 30 minutes.

Step two To make the almond cream, in a large bowl, with a whisk, mix the soft butter to a cream with the icing sugar. Gradually mix in the ground almonds, then the egg, egg yolk and rum or cognac. Mix until smooth, then set aside in the fridge for 30 minutes. Meanwhile, preheat the oven to 180°C/ 350°F/gas 4.

Step three Place one disc of pastry on a baking sheet lined with baking parchment. Spoon the almond cream into the centre. With a palette knife, spread the cream into an even circle, leaving a 4cm (1½ in) border all round. Brush a little of the beaten glaze over the border and carefully drape the other circle of pastry neatly on top, pressing gently on the edge to seal it. With the back of a knife, score the outside edge of the pastry all around (this will completely seal the two rounds of pastry and also make an attractive presentation).

Step four Brush the top of the galette with some more of the beaten glaze (ensure that you do not brush egg yolk on the outside edge of the galette or it will prevent the puff pastry rising), then chill for 10 minutes, so it has time to dry; repeat again to give a richer colour. Now you can use your artistic flair. With the side of a fork or knife, starting from the centre of the galette, score a spiral to the edge of the pastry. Repeat this to achieve an attractive design (if you feel unsure, you could simply make criss-cross lines). Bake for 45 minutes, until golden brown.

Serves 4

500g (1 lb 2oz) shop-bought puff pastry

1 large egg yolk, beaten with 1 tsp water, to glaze

for the almond cream

75g (3oz) unsalted butter, softened

75g (3oz) icing sugar

75g (3oz) ground almonds

1 large egg, plus 1 large egg yolk

1 tbsp dark rum or cognac

Dark Chocolate Mousse with Orange

This dessert must be prepared a few hours in advance to allow it to set in the fridge.

Serves 6

special equipment

6 individual mousse dishes or ramekins (optional)

200g (7oz) best-quality extra bitter chocolate, grated (85 per cent cocoa solids)

8 egg whites, plus 3 egg yolks

75g (3oz) caster sugar

1 tsp finely grated orange zest

¼ tsp finely grated lemon zest

40ml (1½ fl oz) Cointreau

to serve

madeleines or Hot Orange Buns (see page 200)

Step one Break the chocolate into pieces into a bowl. Place the bowl over a pan of simmering water or in a bain-marie at 40°C (104°F) and, on a low heat, melt the chocolate. Cool slightly.

Step two Beat the egg whites until they form soft peaks. Add the sugar a little at a time, whisking until firm peaks are formed.

Step three Stir the egg yolks, citrus fruit zests and Cointreau, if using, into the melted chocolate. Briskly whisk one-third of the whipped egg white into the chocolate mixture, then fold the remainder in very gently. Pour the chocolate mousse into individual dishes, or one large dish. Place in the fridge and allow to set for at least 2 hours. When set, serve with madeleines or Hot Orange Buns (see page 200).

10 9 8 7 6 5 4 3

Published in 2012 by BBC Books, an imprint of Ebury Publishing. A Random House Group company.

Recipes © Raymond Blanc 2012
Book design © Woodlands Books Ltd 2012
All recipes contained in this book first appeared in *Blanc Mange* (1994), *Foolproof French Cookery* (2002) and *A Taste of My Life* (2008).

BBC Books would like to thank Transworld for kind permission to reproduce recipes from *A Taste of My Life* (Bantam Press 2008).

Raymond Blanc has asserted his right to be identified as the author of this Work in accordance with the Copyright, Designs and Patents Act 1988

The Random House Group Limited Reg. No. 954009

A CIP catalogue record for this book is available from the British Library

The Random House Group Limited supports the Forest Stewardship Council® (FSC®), the leading international forest-certification organisation. Our books carrying the FSC label are printed on FSC®-certified paper. FSC is the only forest-certification scheme supported by the leading environmental organisations, including Greenpeace. Our paper procurement policy can be found at www.randomhouse.co.uk/environment

Addresses for companies within the Random House Group can be found at www.randomhouse.co.uk

To buy books by your favourite authors and register for offers visit www.randomhouse.co.uk

Printed and bound in the UK by Butler, Tanner and Dennis Ltd
Colour origination by AltaImage

Commissioning Editor: Muna Reyal
Project Editor: Laura Higginson
Designer: Lucy Stephens
Photographer: Jean Cazals © Woodlands Books Ltd 2012 (see also credits below)
Food Stylists: Marie Ange Lapierre, Katie Giovanni and Julia Azzarello
Prop stylist: Sue Rowlands and Lucy Harvey
Copy Editor: Marion Moisy
Production: Rebecca Jones

Photography: 6, 9, 12, 19, 23, 24, 27, 32, 35, 36, 54, 61, 65, 73, 74, 81, 82, 86, 90, 93, 94, 98, 105, 106, 118, 133, 141, 153, 154, 157, 158, 170, 173, 177, 181, 182, 186, 189, 194, 202 © Jean Cazals 2002

ISBN: 978 1 849 90435 3

MIX
Paper from
responsible sources
FSC
www.fsc.org   FSC® C023561